Jason Warren

Jason Warren is a London-based theatre director, dramaturg and practitioner. His work as a director and dramaturg includes *Nerve/Jekyll and Hyde* (UK tour), *The Sacred Obscene* (London and Edinburgh), *Two Girls* (Southwark Playhouse), and fourteen new plays under the banner of his previous company, AXIS Arts, focused exclusively on new writing, innovative formats and emerging artists. Under AXIS Arts and its predecessor AXIS Theatre he produced the majority of his immersive work, including *Caligula*, *Anima* and *#MSND*. He also works regularly with marginalised voices, including work with disabled artists and in ex-conflict zones.

Jason's work has been reviewed variously as 'muscular and intelligent' and 'disconcertingly nihilistic'. He enjoys sharing these qualities in his work as a regular director at East 15 Acting School. *Creating Worlds* is his first published book.

The **Making Theatre** series of practical handbooks introduces theatre-makers, directors, students and audiences to the key concepts, principles and techniques for making popular styles of contemporary theatre. Each book is written by a working practitioner, drawing on their own experience in the field.

CREATING WORLDS
How to Make Immersive Theatre
Jason Warren

TELLING THE TRUTH
How to Make Verbatim Theatre
Robin Belfield

The publisher welcomes suggestions for further titles in the series.

Jason Warren

Creating Worlds

How to Make Immersive Theatre

NICK HERN BOOKS
London
www.nickhernbooks.co.uk

A Nick Hern Book

Creating Worlds: How to Make Immersive Theatre
first published in Great Britain in 2017
as a paperback original by Nick Hern Books Limited,
The Glasshouse, 49a Goldhawk Road, London W12 8QP

Cover image: Punchdrunk's *Tunnel 228* © Jeff Moore

Designed and typeset by Nick Hern Books, London
Printed and bound in Great Britain by
Ashford Colour Press, Gosport, Hampshire

A CIP catalogue record for this book
is available from the British Library

ISBN 978 1 84842 445 6

MIX
Paper | Supporting
responsible forestry
FSC
www.fsc.org   FSC® C011748

Contents

Introduction

Immersive theatre has been my obsession for a long, long time. My belief in its potential comes from my background. I didn't grow up reciting Shakespeare, I didn't go to theatre school straight after completing A levels and I certainly never had teenage aspirations of directing at the National. As an artist, my influences have often come from outside the theatrical canon. I believe theatre can make us feel how I did when I first listened to my favourite album as a teenager. I believe it can draw us in like the most choice-laden role-playing video game. I'm convinced it can rouse passions *and make the audience express them* like the fiercest political argument after too many beers.

If you ask five artists what immersive theatre is, you might get five different answers. In this introduction we'll talk in detail about what the term really means, but something that most people would agree on is that it's a form that gives the audience greater access to the performance. Whether through roaming freely around the space or talking directly with the characters, these productions invite the audience to take a greater role, to be more involved, to become part of the artistry rather than just spectators.

This book, however, is not a dry analysis of what I think immersive has been. It's not a rundown of performances that have happened in the past. It's written for theatre-makers, artists and students who want to *create* this kind of work. It's also for those who are interested in the guts and ideas that fuel the performances they love. If this book inspires you to create your own performances *and* is enjoyable to read, then I will have achieved my aim.

The joy of working in immersive theatre is that there is so much left to discover. What you're holding in your hands is the fruit of my experiments and projects over the last few years, but I'm also truly excited about the discoveries yet to be made. It's a privilege to be working in a field that's so uncharted, where every project is an opportunity to do something truly innovative. Through monumental mistakes and totally unexpected successes, I've ended up with a philosophy on what makes good immersive theatre. My aim is to help you craft your own beliefs – and to create responsive and rich worlds of your own.

What is Immersive Theatre?

Before we begin creating immersive work, we really should decide what immersive theatre is. It's on everyone's lips. Every five minutes, a new 'immersive' event is announced and sells out – and if you've been to a few of these, you'll know that they often have very few similarities to each other.

I've been to interactive stories where I was locked in a room with twenty-five other people forced to make a moral decision that would change the story;[1] controlled a small island as I struggled to remain independent against the superpowers trying to coerce me into giving up my uranium;[2] been chased by shadowy creatures in the dark underneath London;[3] and watched my mythological parents descend into a murderous feud.[4] All of them were heralded as immersive productions, and none of them bore any resemblance to each other. There was no one type of space unifying the productions. In some the audience were confined to one room, in some they were free to

1. *101: Betrayal*, ONEOHONE Theatre Co., 2011
2. *Archipelago*, Hobo Theatre, 2014
3. *...And Darkness Descended*, Punchdrunk, 2011
4. *Hotel Medea*, Zecora Ura, 2012

roam. Sometimes we could affect the story, at others we were purely spectators. All of them, however, are immersive.

There are common threads I see in all productions that we call immersive. All these productions are (or try to be) innovative in two areas: the role of the audience and how they use the theatre space. Within these threads there's endless variations in both intention and success, but we can make certain general assumptions. It's unlikely that the audience will be sat down in rows facing a stage. We probably don't expect the audience to stay silent throughout then applaud at the end. The actors are not, in all likelihood, separated from the audience by an invisible 'fourth wall' at the edge of the stage. The problem is that we can point at endless examples of productions that are *not* immersive, and sometimes it seems like the form is defined by negatives; that by identifying everything that *isn't* immersive, we can use what's left behind as our definition.

I think this is unhelpful. To me, immersive theatre is about the certain spirit with which we make a performance. A production becomes immersive when it is made by a company who will experiment with the theatrical format in ways that are designed to drag the audience further in. So, for this book, let us agree to drop the debate about definitions and genres. Your production will be immersive, because you have decided it will be. All being well, it will be unlike any immersive theatre we've yet seen.

That being the case, I encourage you to look beyond the current definitions. Create your own terminology, and define your new art form with words that truly cut to the heart of what you're creating. There is already a backlash against this possibly meaningless word, 'immersive'. What is *your* medium? Interactive Theatre, Dilemma Theatre, Alternate World Exhibit... As, so often, we can do better than using the vocabulary we've been given.

Current Forms

It's probably helpful to have an overview of the work that has already been created and described as immersive. It's a vast and diverse field, taking in work of many kinds; all immersive productions are different from each other, but we can draw distinctions between certain families of them. Identifying where you sit on this spectrum can help you to keep your focus, or even help you decide you want to break the mould and do something totally new.

Broadly speaking, we can identify four different varieties of immersive work. I refer to these as Exploration Theatre, Guided Experiences, Interactive Worlds and Game Theatre. These aren't established terms that you'll necessarily see used elsewhere; they're helpful definitions I use that make it easier to be specific when we talk about immersive work. Let's look at each of them in turn.

Exploration Theatre

This is the form that leaps to the minds of the average theatregoer when they hear the word 'immersive'. It's the form that has been pioneered and perfected by Punchdrunk (arguably the most renowned immersive company in the world) over the years, and probably the form that gets the most press. Exploration Theatre melds a traditional theatre experience with a mobile audience and huge attention to the setting they roam around. Crucially, these pieces can, theoretically, exist without an audience. Like a mainstream proscenium-arch production, the piece has been set and rehearsed; it doesn't rely on the audience to propel it forwards and, artistically speaking, can take place no matter what the ticket sales are like.

Generally taking place in a multi-room space, these pieces will present a theatrical experience in multiple places (possibly all at once). The audience is free to explore the space, which is usually intricately designed and a pleasure to be in regardless of the cast's actions, and they can follow whatever strands of the story they wish. Interaction between cast and audience can happen, and sometimes there's a lot of it – but these interactions don't shape the story of the piece. These are logistically easier to plan, as the audience can't do much to derail the piece (though we should never underestimate their capacity for mischief). In some examples (again, notably Punchdrunk) the audience may even be masked. This can have the dual effects of both reducing the amount of verbal interaction *and* anonymising the audience so that they feel more comfortable in this new experience.

Theatre of this nature might have a free-roaming audience (see most of Punchdrunk's work) or the audience may be guided through the performance space in a predetermined order. If you wish to create a piece like this, you'll need to give a huge amount of consideration to the design of the space – not just its artistic merit, but also because of the huge impact it can have on the audience's psychology and their willingness to explore. In Chapter 2: Living Spaces, I've put together a buffet of techniques for you to choose from.

Guided Experiences

At the polar opposite end of the scale we have Guided Experiences. These pieces rely entirely upon the audience, as they are guided through a story that gives them (ideally) countless opportunities to interact and make (again, ideally) meaningful choices.

One of the most well-known is *You Me Bum Bum Train*, a huge-scale interactive experience that takes one audience member at a time through a selection of adventures where they take the lead role (*YMBBT* politely ask that people don't give spoilers about their work, so I'm afraid I can't tell you what these are)... but Guided Experiences can also be tiny. OneOhOne presented a piece in Edinburgh where a small group of audience members were given the power to betray or remain loyal to a shadowy woman who made arbitrary demands. The action remained in one small room throughout, with the audience being coopted into a cult as the play went on.

There are two defining traits in these pieces. Firstly, the audience is integral; the piece cannot take place without at least one audience member present. Secondly, the journey they experience is curated. They will experience the space and the story in a set order. If multiple rooms are used, they will proceed through these rooms when they are invited to. Their choices will have weight when they are invited (either overtly or subtly) to make them.

When done well, these are pieces with a taut and honed narrative through which the audience is propelled at a rapid pace. There may occasionally be breathing room or silence, but the audience can't be left without a set scene for long, as there isn't much for them to explore outside the confines of the planned arc. You'll need to make sure the experience you're offering is fulfilling, and never dull enough that the audience start looking to create their own opportunities for exploration.

Interactive Worlds

An Interactive World is free-roaming, allowing the audience to move through the space however they wish. It also gives weight to their actions and choices, often to the extent of allowing them to influence the end of the story. There is usually a narrative arc underpinning the performance, but this arc is open to change through the audience's choices. Essentially, an Interactive World combines aspects from both of the previous two forms, and becomes markedly more complex because of this.

Unlike Guided Experiences, the possible influence of the audience is limitless. It isn't contained to pre-scripted options and choices. There needs to be enough interesting elements in the space to allow the audience a rewarding exploration, and the cast simultaneously need to be very comfortable improvising *and* know the plot of the play inside out. This is, by far, the most challenging form to plan and execute well, as it requires simultaneously using every technique from the other forms of immersive theatre. Hiding the nuts and bolts of the performance and its structure can become a titanic job. Because of these logistical challenges, it's a form you don't often see happening – though my belief is that we can streamline this process. With planning and a little help from this book, you can start crafting Interactive Worlds today.

Because this form of theatre requires techniques from all the other forms, I'll often seem to assume that you're interested in creating an Interactive World – this avoids me having to repeatedly write 'but don't worry if this isn't relevant to your production'. There's no assumption that these pieces are somehow 'better' or what you *should* be striving to create.

Game Theatre

Game Theatre is an odd beast, and in some ways it can seem opposed to the rest of the types we've mentioned. In my opinion it doesn't really belong under the term 'immersive theatre', as its aims and techniques are entirely different (though equally interesting). Though this is a generalisation, Game Theatre tends to highlight the rules and Mechanics of the performance, rather than hide them behind the narrative. The intention is often to ask participants to engage critically with the world around them by drawing attention to its otherwise unnoticed structures. Other types of Game Theatre exist to explore the spirit of competition between participants, using the Mechanics as a way of specifying how we can succeed within the performance. However, nearly every single piece of Game Theatre I've participated in or heard of has, at some stage, had the immersive label applied, so it's definitely a format worth looking at.

In Game Theatre, the Mechanics *are* the experience. This can be an immensely powerful tool, and my most powerful experience of this was during Hobo Theatre's *The Lowland Clearances*. We'll deal briefly with this form's unique demands in a later chapter.

About This Book

That's quite enough about what already exists – this book is here to help you create the piece that's *going to* exist because of your hard work. This book is broken up into five chapters. **Chapter 1: Starting Out** helps to hone in on what kind of piece you want to make. After that, each chapter focuses on a different set of challenges and opportunities you need to consider when creating your own immersive theatre. You can dip in to them in any order you like, though remember that I may sometimes refer to concepts introduced in an earlier chapter. A glossary at the end is on hand to give you a quick reference to the terminology if you need a reminder. Terms in the glossary will be indicated throughout the book by being capitalised (Like This).

Chapter 2: Living Spaces encourages you to innovate how you use a freely moving audience in your production. We go far beyond simply saying 'you can go anywhere' and start looking at how this freedom of movement can be used to your benefit. We talk about subtly influencing the audience's movements, how to Split and rejoin audience groups organically and how to use your space to create gut-level emotional effects. Whether you're planning a huge multi-room exploration or a tightly honed single-room story, the work in this chapter will help you craft your environment.

Chapter 3: Living Choices focuses on the thorny boundary between audience free will and uncontrolled chaos. We discuss how to 'cast' your audience, making them a functioning and enjoyable part of your piece with their own role to play. We show how to encourage confused or shy participants out of their shell – as well as how to bring unruly ones subtly back into line!

Chapter 4: Living Rehearsals brings things back to the rehearsal room. There are techniques to help you manage the huge complexity of rehearsals along with exercises that prepare your cast for the unexpected. It's all compiled in a helpful schedule, designed to get the most out of the limited time within which we often have to work.

Chapter 5: Living Beyond the Performance takes us outside of the live event. There's a whole world of opportunities to expand your production into the living rooms of your audience and the streets on which they live. This chapter looks at how we do that, as well as how these opportunities can get your audience marketing your play for you.

What This Book Isn't

This is not a set of instructions on how to direct, act or produce in the conventional sense. *Creating Worlds* is concerned with the additional requirements and unique challenges that immersive theatre *adds* to the theatre-making process.

Much of this book assumes a certain level of familiarity with the basic concepts of theatre. You don't need to be an acclaimed actor or director to understand and use the ideas within, but you do need to have grasped the core concepts of performance. For example, I won't address how to play a character in a production, but I *will* talk about how you can give your scripted character an interactive life that makes unscripted interactions with the audience possible. I won't go into the basics of how to use lighting in a theatrical production, but I'll talk about how you can influence a free-roaming audience to go where you want them to go by using light.

This book is designed to be 'methodology-agnostic'; I don't expect you to be working from a background of Stanislavsky, Brecht, Artaud, Littlewood or anyone else. The techniques in *Creating Worlds* can be applied to your art no matter what it's based on.

1. Starting Out

Your Mission Statement

It's nearly time to get some basic concepts under our belt, then move on and apply them to our immersive productions. But first... You need to decide what you're trying to create.

You know you want to make a piece of immersive theatre. You may have seen what's out there, and how much the form varies from company to company, even from piece to piece. You probably have an idea of what you like and dislike in an immersive performance. So the first, and most important, question is: What kind of experience are you making? It's a broad question, but a fundamental one.

For starters, decide what the single most important aspect of your piece would be for your audience. Sum it up in one sentence. Here are some examples:

'I want the audience to be totally overwhelmed by the amount of experiences they can choose between.'

'I want to create a world so convincing that the audience forgets they're experiencing a play.'

'I want the audience's choices to have real consequences.'

'I want to give the audience a total sensory overload.'

You can incorporate any ideas you like, but let's face it: immersive theatre is hard. Your time, your resources and your actors are going to be stretched to their limit, so knowing where your focus is right from the outset is going to make your life a lot easier (or at least more tolerable) when you're trying to make hard decisions further down the line. It's also going to keep you motivated when things get chaotic. Having that clear Mission Statement in your head for the genre-smashing interactive world you are planning is going to give you that extra drive to push through those late nights of thinking and writing.

So go and scribble. Make increasingly absurd and maniacal statements about what you're looking to achieve. And when you've got the perfect sentence, that phrase that boils your dream immersive piece down to its core guiding principle, read the next section. We'll start talking about how to achieve it.

Simplicity Works

Counter-intuitive, isn't it? Who on earth, if they believe in simplicity, would try to create an immersive piece of theatre? Fair point, you're about to embark upon a very un-simple journey. To make your journey of creation possible, there are some things that can stay simple and act as your compass. The most important of these is your Mission Statement.

Take a well-known example: Punchdrunk have been one of the foremost names in immersive theatre for many years (for very good reason). They make a very specific kind of immersive, where the world of the story is the most important aspect of the work. Audience choice doesn't play a huge role in their pieces. It's totally free-roaming, but it largely makes no difference what an audience member does. The play remains the same. This isn't a weakness; Punchdrunk know right down to their bones what they're trying to achieve. What they create in their Exploration Theatre pieces already stretches the limits of what is achievable in any rehearsal period, and if they tried to incorporate every possible aspect of immersive theatre, their work would be both unfocused *and* under-rehearsed.

So guard that Mission Statement carefully. For every decision you make, *especially* when it's about incorporating something new into the play, you need to weigh it against your goal. Does it help you achieve that holy grail you set out to find right at the start? Often the answer is no.

Focused pieces work brilliantly. I've seen pieces centred around the audience's ability to influence the story that took place within one bare room (OneOhOne, a small company from Oxford, do this admirably). All the effort had gone into a multi-stranded set of decisions that made me agonise over my every action. In Zecura Ura's *Hotel Medea*, I had very little choice in what I did or where I went, and the world was small... but I was totally dragged into the storyline. The immediacy of the writing and intensity of the actors meant my own little desires and urges would have been irrelevant anyway!

Know what you're creating. It's going to make life a lot easier later on.

Concepts

Throughout the book, you'll notice words that are capitalised: Like This. This means that it's a key concept I work with, one that I'll probably come back to a few times in the book. Some of these are, as far as I know, unique, and I've had to come up with brief descriptive names for them. Hopefully, this will leave us with a shared vocabulary that will both make reading the book smoother *and* facilitate your own discussions as you create your work. In many cases, giving these concepts a concrete name also helps to refine our thinking even further. There's a glossary of all these terms at the end of the book, but they're first introduced in the chapter that makes most sense. If you're reading the book out of order and come across a word that seems odd, refer to the glossary – it's probably been covered in an earlier section.

There are three concepts I want to put forward right at the start. These are Elegance, Rewards and Flavour.

Elegance

One of my buzzwords for good immersive theatre is Elegance.

What this really means is that the piece is 'mechanically invisible'; the audience can't see the planning put into the piece, they don't feel artificially railroaded and they are never fully aware that the piece is rigidly structured and timetabled.

Too often, the audience is bludgeoned into action. A guard in a gas mask bellows 'MOVE!', and everyone sighs in resignation as they shuffle to the next room, aware it's time for the next scene. There's no feeling of organic life, only a series of instructions thinly disguised by costume and dialogue.

I think we can and should be more inventive (or devious) than that. I'll be giving you ideas for how to create a piece that never feels artificial. You'll be running your show with attention to detail and meticulous planning, but your audience will never directly be aware of it.

I'll be referring to Elegance repeatedly in this book. To me, it's one of the principal concepts I'll put forward that everyone should be aspiring to. Respect the hard work you're putting in; never let the audience reach the limits of the world you've created. They should always feel that if they explored through one more door or asked one more question they would discover another part of your devised world.

Rewards

Another of the core concepts I'll ask you to work with is the Reward. This is essentially how you train your audience to interact fully with your performance. By rewarding the type of behaviour that helps your play along, the audience will swiftly understand their role in your piece. It's more Elegant than reading out a list of rules or having an out-of-character team member encouraging them. It's a *lot* more Elegant than having a character give a clunky 'in-character' encouragement to interact.

The essence of a Reward is that you, as a company, anticipate how an audience might interact. You consider where they might 'explore', be that a physical exploration of the space or a verbal exploration by talking to a character. Your job is to make sure that there is something waiting for them at the other side of that exploration. You will have placed an interesting scene or object in a hidden space, or an incendiary piece of backstory that can only be found by asking the actors questions. Make the audience feel that their endeavours have importance early on in the performance. Later on, when the stakes are higher and there's less time for hand-holding the audience, they'll have already learned the rules of your piece.

Flavour

I use the word Flavour to denote an immersive element that has no function within the play other than making the world feel richer. A character's diary found in the space, while fascinating, may not be necessary to make the play operate. Don't overlook these Flavour additions. If the audience starts to feel that every conversation, object and room is necessary, the joy of discovery will be overtaken by a sense of 'Okay, how do I use this then?' Allow pure exploration to be its own Reward in some cases.

Some General Advice

With those concepts understood, you hopefully have an idea of what it is you're going to start building. Stay aware of why you've chosen to create immersive theatre – and your Mission Statement that reminds you of the effect you want to have on your audience. This point of reference is your anchor, the ideal against which you should measure every idea you start toying with. That guiding sentence you came up with at the beginning of your process will stay vitally important right up to the day you sit down after the last performance and consider the success of the show.

One of my first immersive pieces, *Anima*, was born of a desire to make the audience culpable; to make them share the responsibility for, and satisfaction in, the play's outcome. I had been inspired by the depth of choice that modern computer role-playing games offer the player, and wanted to explore that level of interaction with a live audience. Keeping hold of that guiding principle meant that I was able to retain focus. When I was tempted to invest time and energy into complex set, long tracts of dialogue or any other resource-draining idea, I could ask myself whether they furthered my core goal. Often, they didn't. These abandoned ideas ended up being secreted away in my notebooks, ready for a production that would use them to greater effect.

If you're reading this as an individual actor or director rather than as a member of a group (be it a group of students or an acting company), you will also need to get a good team around you from the outset and to define who has responsibility for certain areas of the production. The huge number of elements to keep track of in immersive work might demand a change in your usual working patterns, so have an honest look at how you tend to operate. If you're prone to micromanaging and keeping a tight hold of every aspect of your productions, learning to let go will be a lifesaver. There's just too much to keep track of in an immersive piece for any one person. I speak from experience, as I was that kind of director prior to my first immersive work! I fought tooth and nail to keep on top of it all myself, making my first piece much harder than it needed to be. By learning to let go, your production won't just be easier to manage; ensuring your collaborators feel ownership in the work will make their contributions far more creative and insightful.

Conversely, if you've tended to work in a free-form, collaborative way (perhaps as part of a devised company), you may have to put some boundaries around the process. Generate ideas together and pool your creativity, but make sure one or two people are keeping tabs on each area. As your multi-stranded narratives spiral ever-outward, as your design elements multiply, tasks will need to be centralised under one person. The entire web of narrative choices (for example) should be at the fingertips of one person so they can easily spot problems and conflicts.

It's not my place to tell you how to delegate different roles; this will be influenced by the kind of people you are and the kind of production you're creating. It might be that one person handles designing the space while another works on interactions with the audience, or it might be that one person is handling the creation of the main storyline while another adds Flavour. You know your requirements better than I do, so make whatever choices you need – as long as you have actually *made* those choices.

You will do well so long as you remember that this may be the biggest job you've ever taken on. It's bigger than any one person, and by working together in a disciplined way you will hopefully create something incredible.

Case Studies

As we're discussing theoretical ideas throughout this book, I've chosen to include practical examples so you can understand these concepts in practice. I'll be making reference to four immersive productions I've been involved in and showing you how our topics were applied to those examples. These productions were all vastly different in nature, and I've chosen them to give you a real variety of outcomes and objectives. These aren't meant as an instruction to copy those examples; the possibilities for your play are limitless and I could fill five books with examples if I were so inclined... and I would still fail to serve up the perfect idea for your piece. That can only come from you.

Below is a brief overview of these four pieces, laid out so you can understand what their unique tone and aims were.

#MSND

#MSND was an immersive rendering of Shakespeare's *A Midsummer Night's Dream* created by my production company, AXIS Arts. It transferred the setting from a forest to a seedy nightclub, recasting the characters accordingly. Oberon became the shady character doing deals behind the scenes, vaguely implicated in drugs and prostitution. Puck became his 'enforcer', Titania the most prestigious dancer, and Bottom a hapless clubgoer.

Taking place within one large space, our aim was to have the audience act as if in a real nightclub. We used a genuine club in a reclaimed South London factory as our setting. A live DJ provided the soundtrack for the evening, and the bar was serving throughout the performance. The action of the play was divided between free-roaming segments where the cast interacted with the audience, and scripted-dialogue set pieces that progressed the plot.

The piece was interactive, but the narrative was set and we used Shakespeare's original text – the audience did not influence the story in any way. It functioned like a small-scale piece of Exploration Theatre and was designed to accommodate as many audience members as the space would hold.

Anima

Anima was my first Interactive World. It cast the audience as survivors of a plague that was sweeping the country. When they purchased their tickets, they received an information pack in the post. That pack, comprised of documents seemingly created within our fictional world, informed them of their role and the world they were entering. It confirmed that they had signed up for a 'disaster insurance package' with Osiris Corporation, along with a wealth of Osiris propaganda.

The play was designed to pit the audience in a series of dilemmas that forced them to choose between equally questionable moral Paths. As the story progressed, they would find themselves choosing (or being coerced into) an alliance with either the Osiris Corporation or a group of terrorists called the Network. Depending on the actions of the audience, one of four drastically different endings could occur – with multiple different minor variations occurring along the route to each ending. We were interested in providing opportunities for audience members to work against each other, and wanted to provide an arena where ideologies and beliefs became more important than friendships.

The space was a collection of buildings belonging to a school, surrounding a playing field. This became the Osiris Corp Quarantine & Research Facility, and the production was designed to accommodate a maximum audience of fifty.

Loveplay

With *Loveplay*, we created a piece of Exploration Theatre. Taking Moira Buffini's script of the same name, we placed it in a cellar complex with multiple rooms and branching corridors. Our setting was a sort of time-travelling dating agency, where audience members ventured away from the agency lounge to explore rooms placed in the last two thousand years of English history. In each of these rooms, a scene from the play would be occurring on a looping schedule. The traditional staging of *Loveplay* consists of ten scenes in chronological order – each showing a different interpretation of love set in the same physical location but two hundred years apart.

Our intention with this piece was to allow freedom of movement and choice whilst ensuring that the audience saw all ten scripted scenes of Moira's play. The audience were free to interact with characters not involved in scripted scenes, but we also needed to preserve the set nature of the text. The performance was designed to accommodate an audience of forty.

Caligula

Caligula is probably my most ambitious project so far. Designed to be an Interactive World and draw on my learnings from *Anima*, it also had to incorporate the set text and ending of Albert Camus' original writing. Our challenge to ourselves was to create a piece that had total freedom of action for the audience, making their choices feel meaningful within the play, but still preserve the scripted ending – essential to the philosophical themes underpinning Camus' work.

This performance also utilised the underground space used for *Loveplay*, and transplanted the setting of *Caligula* from Imperial Rome to a twisted dictatorial London. The audience were cast as low-level senators in a dystopian version of London's government, and we hoped to explore their real political beliefs – though the play did not aim to cast judgement on any set of principles. The audience limit for this piece was roughly thirty.

A Note on Finding Spaces

You might be worried that you could never afford the reclaimed warehouse-turned-nightclubs, schools or underground complexes I mentioned in the case studies. Let me put your mind at ease.

Every single one of these spaces was offered for free.

To be more precise, their owners were always willing to accept something other than money in exchange for us using their space. In the case of the school, the cast and I provided a couple of workshops for their students. The nightclub trusted that we'd fill the room up enough to make a decent profit on the bar. The underground complex gave us the space without any conditions once we sat down and told them our ideas.

You may not always get the space you want, and if it's an established theatre venue you almost certainly won't until you can offer either a chunk of cash or a significant track record for pulling in big audiences and, therefore, money at the box office... but there are *always* interesting and under-utilised locations that will allow you access if you offer something meaningful in return (whether that's workshops, marketing or just the respect and passion of talking to them in-depth about why your piece is worthwhile).

Be as creative in finding your performance's home as you are in creating the piece itself.

What's the Story?

Before you move on from this introductory chapter, there are fundamental questions to answer about the story you're telling. Firstly, where it's coming from: are you adapting an existing story, or are you creating something from the ground up? There are three major ways this can play out.

- You're creating a brand-new story. It may be within an existing world (perhaps set within a Brothers Grimm-style fairy land or the weird horror of H.P. Lovecraft's Cthulhu stories), but the narrative is new. *Anima*, one of our case studies, fits within this category.

- You're making an immersive adaptation of an existing story that uses the original text prominently – three of our case studies, *Caligula*, *Loveplay* and *#MSND*, do this.

- You're using an existing story as a jumping-off point to create something new. Punchdrunk do this in many of their pieces (using tales such as *Dr Faustus* and *Woyzeck* as starting points, but not necessarily using large amounts of the original text).

This choice has an impact on every aspect of your performance, most notably how you use interactivity and the audience's free will. If you've got a story that must end one way, it's a lot harder to craft a piece that the audience can influence. It's not impossible, but it will take careful building. You'll find techniques in Chapter 3: Living Choices, the section on crafting interactions, that will help with this. If you're creating an original story, however, then presumably you'll choose to craft a piece that serves your purposes and your space.

Adapting a Story

When you're adapting an existing piece of art, you're signing up to steer a course between utilising the interactive elements of immersive theatre and honouring the original creator's intentions. Sometimes this is easy; myths, legends and other public domain stories are often so old that their original creator is lost to history. You have relatively free rein with your work, though the audience may have strong expectations.

It becomes more difficult if you start working with stories that are still very much attached to their creator's name. We've all seen poor adaptations of Shakespeare, and the same could be said for Dickens, Chekhov, Dostoevsky... or for any modern author. There are two issues that need addressing right at the beginning of your work. The first, of course, is to check that you can legally acquire permission to use this intellectual property. For many older works, such as Shakespeare, these stories are 'out of copyright' – this means that you can legally present them on stage without needing permission from an agency, writer or organisation. A good rule of thumb is that it may be out of copyright if the writer died over seventy years ago. With the majority of stories from the later twentieth and twenty-first centuries (and some older work too), there is someone who legally owns the rights to the story. In these cases you will need to contact the rights holder, and this information can usually be found by looking in the front of the book or on the reverse of the DVD case.

The second consideration with pre-existing material is the audience's expectations of the story. If we present a piece that draws strongly on the plot of *Romeo and Juliet*, the audience will bring certain powerful ideas into the space. They will expect to see the lovers die tragically, and two warring families. You are free to honour or subvert these expectations as you wish, but if you *do* reject the traditional expectations of a story then make sure the audience is pleasantly surprised rather than unfulfilled.

Once you've dispensed with all these initial considerations, start thinking about the themes of the story you're using. Consider the moral or message of the story. Decide what the 'tone' of the story is. Write all of this down on a sheet of paper, and stick it somewhere you'll see when you're working on your piece. You have a responsibility to make sure your Immersive Additions enhance the audience's experience by complementing the story, rather than degrading the work by using it to carry clumsily made interactive gimmicks. Then, write down the major plot points of the story and divide them into loose scenes, which you will later use as the basis for your production's structure.

As long as you stick to this, the rest of the process is the same as for any other piece (developing character, working with dialogue, considering the actors' physical work, etc).

The Audience

I'll talk a lot about 'the audience' in this book, and make reference to predicting or influencing what they will do in an immersive production. It's important to understand exactly what I mean by this.

When I talk about influencing or predicting the audience, I am talking about the audience *as a group*. There is simply no way at all to predict the actions of an individual person, and our plans become increasingly unreliable as we talk about smaller and smaller groups of individuals. In an audience of a hundred people, I can be fairly confident that 'most people will do this' or 'a small amount of them will do that'. We can Split that audience into groups whilst staying Elegant because crowds tend to react in relatively manageable ways.

There should never be a point in your play where you *need* an individual to make a certain choice. You have the ability to shape certain routes (both literally in the space and figuratively in the story) that groups of people can choose, but remember that this is *all* you can do.

Below is a list of three things you might want to do in an immersive production:

1. Predict, exactly, what the audience will do.

2. Offer the audience significant freedom of choice during the production.

3. Keep the production Elegant.

The problem is, you can only manage two of these at once. Be conscious, always, of this dilemma. My personal preference is to highlight the second and third points, using the first only when I have to. In Chapter 3: Living Choices, we'll talk about ways to keep your audience on the straight and narrow when you need to.

The Spine of the Piece

Have your Mission Statement to hand for this section. Building an immersive production has different demands to building any other sort of play, and you could start from a number of different places. As we mentioned earlier, Chapters 2 to 5 of this book can be read in any order, and deal with different aspects of immersive work. The first decision you'll have to make is what you're going to start planning first – what's the central spine of your piece? Really, it boils down to being one of two things, and the sentence you wrote earlier will tell you which to pick.

For some artists, the big appeal is in creating an aesthetically exciting world for your audience to explore. Stories can grow organically out of the setting you can create. So if you're looking to start from building the perfect imaginary space, begin with Chapter 2: Living Spaces.

For other artists, there's choice. The world and the space, these things will come later. What you're focused on is having a branching and responsive world, where the audience is invited (or forced) to make decisions and feel the piece reshape itself around them. Be aware though – this is the hardest kind to achieve! But if you can cope with sleepless nights surrounded by increasingly illegible scraps of paper and some intensely complex rehearsal schedules, head to Chapter 3: Living Choices.

There are also chapters on the rehearsal process and extending the immersive piece into the build-up to the live performance. I've tried to present the chapters in an order that makes some sense, but inevitably many of these concepts need to occur simultaneously. It would be madness to plan everything to do with the space itself before you even touch on the audience interactions in the story! With that in mind, you've reached the end of the first chapter, and we've established some shared key ideas – now let's dive in to the details.

2. Living Spaces

Beyond Staging

'I can take any empty space and call it a bare stage. A man walks across this empty space whilst someone else is watching him, and this is all that is needed for an act of theatre to be engaged.'

Peter Brook, *The Empty Space*

Any piece of theatre happens in a space. It might be a thirty-seater fringe venue above a pub, the Olivier auditorium at the National Theatre, a disused warehouse or a clearing in a forest; it's a space, and good theatre pays attention to its environment.

When you're putting on an immersive piece, the space becomes an even bigger consideration. Think about how much attention we give to the stage in a traditional production, one where the audience is sat in one place throughout the performance. We can agonise endlessly over sightlines, debate the correct positioning of the set, and spend half an hour deciding whether one particular lighting state is slightly too warm or cold. When we allow the audience to wander throughout that space at will (as is likely the case in Exploration Theatre or an Interactive World), everything has to be considered in even more detail. They might look behind every item of scenery, peer through any door and touch anything they can reach. The space has to be designed from every angle – unlike in other theatre forms, you can't have the running order taped to the back of the scenery. You can't have an actor hovering at the door to listen for their cue.

Creating a space that is totally 'explorable' is hard work. Luckily, it's also hugely enjoyable. This chapter is aimed at helping you manage your space as fully as possible – and hopefully in a way that lends some structure and clarity to a very subjective process. If you do your prep early on, you'll be able to let your imagination run riot later without losing track of the complexities of your immersive piece.

There's two areas to consider: the first will deal with how you work with a single room or area in your space; the other addresses how you get your audience moving between rooms and the journeys they go on.

The Space: Your First Cast Member

Obviously, your performance space should be rich and vibrant, filled with interesting elements to explore and observe... But to take your production to the next level, we should think of the space as more than just a backdrop for the piece. In a well-executed immersive piece, the space is an actor, capable of interacting with and influencing the audience.

We do this by planning how our space can impact the psyche of our audience. How we design and work within a space can have a massive impact on the audience's experience of the play. We can affect their journeys through the space, encouraging them to linger in a space or rush through it. We can influence how they feel about a room, and even where they stand within that room. Crucially, by doing this through the space, we can keep it Elegant. There'll never be any need to instruct the audience and break your immersion.

The space is your secret weapon – and it's a quiet one. If you've used the space well, the audience won't spend time at the end talking about the Mechanics and techniques you applied to it. They'll be talking about the stories they shared there and the sensory experiences they had within it.

How to Use a Room

Each area of your space can be designed to influence the audience's psychology, and in this section we'll be examining how we can do that. Part 1 is about how to utilise individual areas of your entire performance space, helping you to plan their purpose in the performance and work in service of the aims of the piece. We'll look at how you can create claustrophobia, excitement or contentment simply through (for example) the placement of furniture or the positioning of lights. Later, we'll look at how audiences might be coaxed into travelling between different areas of the space.

All the concepts that apply to a traditional theatre production will still hold true here, so I'm not going to talk about the basics of design and set. What we're going to discuss are the unique elements of immersive theatre. Mainly, this involves the unique relationship between the audience and the space.

Planning this relationship in advance is incredibly important; whilst your cast can react in the moment, the space can't. It has to be ready for the chaos your audience can unleash so that your cast has the best possible structure to work in.

Much of what we'll discuss in this chapter is actually to do with psychology rather than pure design. Partly, this is because it's very difficult to have broad brushstrokes about how your piece should be designed when this is totally dictated by your setting. More important, however, is that the space has a unique set of abilities in an immersive piece that no other theatre form allows you to play with to such an extreme extent. Your mobile audience will be influenced by it, and encouraged or discouraged to explore depending on the effects the space has on their subconscious.

This might sound daunting, but don't worry. These concepts are easily understandable.

The Problematic Audience

One of the most frustrating lessons I had in my early immersive projects was that the audience will very often hide at the sides of a room. We've all been educated to believe that theatre is a sacred art that should not be interrupted or disturbed, and audience members unfamiliar with the way immersive theatre works tend to stick to that code of conduct. Trust me, it can kill the atmosphere of your piece. These long-standing and ingrained behaviours don't just affect where the audience stands, but also how likely they are to interact with the production and how much they'll talk to each other.

Case Study: #MSND

When we created #*MSND* (one of our case studies), we had a fantastic nightclub space with a functional bar in a disused warehouse. We couldn't wait to see the audience fill it, dance, get drunk and generally enjoy the phenomenal environment we'd created. It was crushing when the audience, without exception, all stood around the walls. They instinctively created an arena, enclosing the performance space. And it got worse; whenever a character came anywhere near their part of the wall, they politely parted to create space in case that area of the space was going to become a focal performance point.

These traditional behaviours continued, and our audiences resolutely refused to draw attention to themselves. They were not, in any way, surly or hostile; they applauded and laughed throughout the piece, seeming to enjoy it thoroughly as a piece of standard narrative theatre. Unfortunately, much of the later performance relied on having an audience to interact with – so when these moments emerged, the silence in the space was deafening.

We tried everything. By the fourth performance, we were even giving a pre-show speech to encourage interaction. One or two hardy souls briefly stepped into the space now and then, but the crushing weight of forty-nine other audience members staying round the walls soon had them scurrying back into place. In the end, for the fifth performance, we solved the problem... Totally by accident.

There are a number of ways you can subtly direct your audience to use the space whilst keeping the piece Elegant, but first we have to understand what causes the problem. I call it the Void.

The Void

If, at any point, someone in the audience has to cross a large empty space, it could become a Void. If they have to do that in plain view of other audience members, it will almost *certainly* become a Void. If the room is very quiet when they cross, it is, without a shadow of a doubt, a Void. So what is a Void?

It's any large area that unintentionally discourages the audience to enter it. 'Large' is a relative term, and it's unimportant what the actual dimensions are – if it's larger than any other empty area in that room, it's a potential Void. Voids can cause real problems. By encouraging static and passive behaviours, a Void can decrease markedly the power of the scene in which it occurs. Unfortunately, the problems don't end there. Audiences are constantly being taught how an immersive production works (a concept we'll look at in more detail later), and the behaviours learned in a Void will then be taken by the audience into other spaces and scenes.

Frustratingly, you can never pinpoint with total accuracy whether it will become one; until the audience filter into the room, the Void doesn't exist. This is because, really, the Void isn't created by your choices or your space. It's created by the audience.

Somewhat surprisingly, the audience themselves create the dynamic that prevents them from engaging fully with your piece. Throughout this book, I'll show how the audience will build their own rules and stick to them – because of this, it's very difficult to break the Void once it's been created. So, before you allow the audience in... make sure you've Smashed the Void.

Case Study: #MSND

We stumbled on to a way of breaking the Void before it occurred. For totally unrelated reasons, we put a podium in the centre of the space on the fifth performance (it was there to give Puck something to clamber onto during a monologue). When our audience entered the space, there was the the usual filing around the walls – but some of the audience clustered around the podium instead. My producer and I shared an incredulous look, because this made no sense. Despite the reluctance all week to go anywhere that looked like it might be where action occurred, here they were clustered around the most obvious focal point in the space. Something had happened, but we weren't sure what it was.

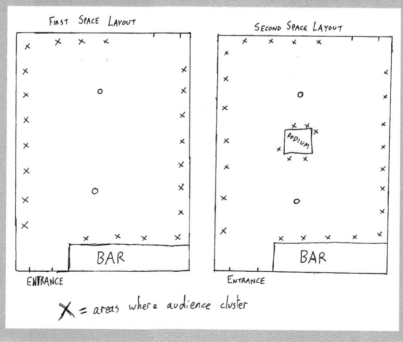

FIRST SPACE LAYOUT

SECOND SPACE LAYOUT

BAR

BAR

ENTRANCE

ENTRANCE

✗ = areas where audience cluster

Overnight, we discussed that it might be something to do with breaking up the space and came up with a plan for the next day. As the podium had broken the space in half, we would use these two halves to experiment with the audience. We left one half as it had been on the previous night, just the wall and the podium on opposite sides of an empty space. In the other half, we placed two tables in the space between wall and podium. The results were beyond anything we expected. In our empty half, the audience behaved as we expected, clustering around wall and podium. In the furnished half, our theory was that they might also cluster around the tables.

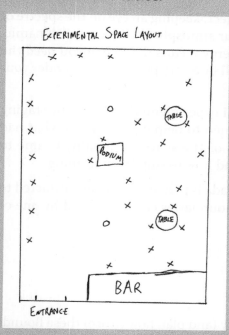

EXPERIMENTAL SPACE LAYOUT

PODIUM

TABLE

TABLE

BAR

ENTRANCE

In the end, they didn't cluster at all. They moved freely in the gaps between wall, tables and podium. They lounged on tables, stood in gaps that contained no objects and even sat on the edge of the podium (staying there even when Puck loomed over them in her monologue). As if this wasn't enough, they also didn't retreat from the action when characters came towards them. It was an entirely different audience, existing in parallel with their companions in the other half of the space.

Over the course of the evening, the pattern continued: free movement in the furnished half, static behaviour in the empty.

The audience from our furnished half would occasionally bring their behaviours into the static group. They walked to their friends in the other group by crossing the empty space rather than scuttling around the walls. Once there, however, they swiftly adopted the static attitude of that half of the space. The reverse was true, with static audience members becoming free and easy once they moved to the cluttered half. Something was at play in the layout of the space, something that worked with the audience's subconscious.

Smashing the Void

When you're planning your project, keeping an eye on the spectre of the Void allows you to keep your atmosphere vibrant and dynamic. Maintaining the audience's energy means that when you *need* the Void (more on that later...) – it'll be a very powerful tool under your control.

During the year after #*MSND*, I experimented regularly by staging small 'laboratory' events designed to help me figure out what had happened in those two halves of the space. Gradually, I came to understand how Voids work, and how to stop them forming.

The fundamental discovery I made is that audiences are attracted to the Boundaries of the space. Boundaries can be created by one of three factors:

1. Objects

2. Light

3. Action

If you don't learn how to identify (and plan how to use) these Boundaries, they will be a real hindrance to you... but when you *do* know what they are, they also become the tool you use to Smash the Void. Before we look at how to work with those Boundaries, however, there's another concept you need to understand: Zones.

Zones

A Zone is an area of the space that shares a Boundary. In our #*MSND* example above, the space started with one Zone (a large space bounded by four walls). When we put the podium in, it divided the space into two Zones. Bear in mind that the Boundaries may not be totally solid. A row of narrowly spaced chairs would define a Zone just as clearly as a wall. It's a nebulous thing, and slightly down to interpretation, but you should be able to make fairly clear decisions about whether an area you're looking at has one Zone or two (or more). The average space will contain one Zone, but some more interesting spaces already have Features that divide them into two or more before you make any design choices. Commonly, these might include a raised section of flooring or an archway.

I said earlier that a certain area might turn into a Void. To be truly specific, Voids form out of individual Zones. They exist only within that Zone, and don't stretch into another. If it seems like you have one massive Void stretching across your multi-room space, this is actually several independent Voids sitting next to each other, each of which will need to be smashed with different tactics.

Therefore it seems logical that when you've identified your Zones you will have also identified your potential Voids. You may remember that I said a Void doesn't exist until the audience themselves create it, so you may be wondering how we can predict the existence of a Void before the audience enter the space. Well, now that you understand a little about Zones we can be a little more precise about how Voids can emerge:

- Audiences create Voids by bringing a combination of traditional theatregoer behaviours and social anxiety into an immersive production.

- The more intimidating a Zone is, the more likely an audience member will be to revert to this 'safe' and ingrained behaviour.

If we look at what makes a Zone intimidating, we can begin to predict the likelihood of a Void emerging in one.

LIVING SPACES

We need to be clear by what we mean by 'intimidating'; what we're talking about here is a very social fear, the fear of drawing attention to oneself in an embarrassing way. Much of the embarrassment a new immersive audience member experiences actually comes from a fear that they will somehow behave in a way that is 'wrong'. If we're fair, we have to admit that this fear is valid; there is no more cringeworthy disaster than forgetting to put your phone on silent and having a text alert blare out in a suspenseful silence during the pivotal monologue of a production – and that's a rule we *already know*. Imagine, then, the fear that assaults the audience when they find themselves asked to operate according to a totally new code of conduct.

So if this is the kind of intimidation that will nudge an audience into creating a Void, we need to design our Zones in a way that minimises this risk. That's not to say that we can't create atmospheres of fear in our productions – we can absolutely evoke the atmospheric horror required by a performance of *Dracula* whilst still smashing the social horror of a Void.

Predicting Voids

The first step is to decide where your Zones actually are. Take a look at the rooms in your space – being there physically is the best way of doing so, but even sketching a ground plan on a napkin would help! As I mentioned earlier, this isn't an exact science so you will need to rely on your gut feeling. Which areas of a performance space feel self-contained and independent? Many rooms, when stripped of furniture, form one single Zone, but if there are pillars or built-in Features (like a bar or raised area) then these might break a room into multiple Zones.

Make a note of the Zones you're working with, assigning them a letter or number so you can refer to them easily later on.

With your Zones worked out, you can start predicting the potential Voids. Start from the largest Zone and work downwards (as the larger Zones are more likely to create Voids). Every Zone is unique, and there's no replacement for your intuition as a theatre-maker, but there are some common risk factors that you can use as a starting point. Remember, you're essentially identifying Zones that could cause that gut-level fear of embarrassment in an audience member.

Imagine two audience members on opposite sides of the Zone. If they would have to raise their voices to talk to each other, the space has Void potential! Relatively few people like to raise their voices before someone else has, so if your audience are discouraged from talking, the ensuing silence will contribute towards creating a Void. If this is true across both the length *and* width of the Zone, it's even more of a risk.

The placement of the entry into the Zone is important, and if the audience is greeted with a large empty space directly in front of them they will tend to scuttle along the walls instead – creating a Void. This initial introduction to a Zone is important, and if the audience accidentally creates a fourth wall between themselves and the rest of the Zone then they'll tend to keep it there.

A way to visualise the potential risk of a Void forming is to imagine that everything in the space has Gravity. The biggest objects (set pieces, walls, etc.) have the most Gravity, and close objects exert a greater Pull than distant objects. Familiar objects (such as red-velvet audience seating) exert a greater Pull than obvious 'props' (such as a throne). Audiences will react to that Gravity, getting pulled towards the elements of the space that exert the greatest attraction. They'll keep getting pulled by that Gravity until they find a place they can claim as their own – often the nearest available patch of wall. If this process ends up leading them around the walls of the space, forming an arena, then you will have a very hard time getting someone to step into the middle of that Zone with all audience eyes upon them. You will have a Void on your hands.

When you're designing the set or layout for your space, consider these Zones. Without destroying the artistic integrity of your piece, ask yourself how you can lessen the likelihood of a Void forming. Careful placement of even a small prop can make a big impact, as I'll show in the next section when we look at Physical Boundaries.

Physical Boundaries

Physical Boundaries are the easiest to understand and construct. They exist in a space before you start creating your piece, and no matter what you do they will continue to exist. Your only options are to accept the Boundaries that exist already or to redefine them according to your desires.

Physical Boundaries are any structures or items that define a playing area. Commonly, you will initially encounter these in your space as walls, fences or vegetation. They tell us where the playing space (and the specific Zones within it) begin and end, and they separate Zones from each other. Two characters standing ten metres away from each other in a large room are, in terms of their ability to interact, closer to each other than characters standing ten centimetres apart on the opposite sides of a wall. This sounds obvious, something we take for granted... but understanding exactly how Physical Boundaries work on our psyches is vital if we wish to use them for our own ends. Delving briefly into pop psychology, we can suppose that Physical Boundaries are comforting to the audience. We have always existed within them. Our homes have defined Physical Boundaries, and the rooms within our homes have defined Physical Boundaries. We use Boundaries to define the functions of spaces – even an open-plan kitchen/dining room/lounge will generally have a clear delineation between which part of the space is used for which function. Structure and order are comforting, because they tell us how to behave. It's possibly worth noting that for hundreds of years the mainstream world of theatre has had the edge of the stage and the arms of the audience's seats as very clear Physical Boundaries.

The same will be true in your production. Your audience will often feel pulled to the Boundaries of the space where they feel most comfortable, out of view and away from the action. If this is an indoor space, it will commonly be the walls. As you know from the last section, this is the audience responding to the Gravity of these objects.

If you want to change this behaviour, you need to use this Gravity to your advantage! When we put our podium in the middle of the space in *#MSND*, we did two things. Firstly, we broke the space into two

Zones, giving a Void less room to exist (remember, large empty spaces increase the feeling of social embarrassment). Secondly, we put a large object in the space that had its own Gravity, pulling people towards it (this object was nondescript and plain enough that it didn't immediately look like a 'prop' or item of scenery). Later, when we put chairs and tables in one of the Zones, putting that amount of Gravity in the Zone meant that the audience felt comfortable wandering freely. They were always heading towards something safe.

There are two broad aspects you need to consider with your Physical Boundaries. First, what effect will the pre-existing Physical Boundaries have? How, for example, will the walls of the space affect the audience? Once that's worked out, you can start to decide whether you'll alter the Physical Boundaries of the space. There are myriad ways of doing this, but here are some examples:

- Hanging cloth or groundsheets from the roof can create new walls, firmly dividing one Zone into two. Be aware that how you use the hanging material can make it look either like a wall or like the backcloth of a stage. The latter will repel your audiences away, due to their ingrained 'stay out of the play's way' behaviour.

- A row of furniture (blocks, chairs, a bar, etc.) can divide a Zone into two whilst still allowing the ability to see into the neighbouring Zone. This can encourage movement between Zones, which we'll cover later.

- Scattering furniture or large objects throughout the Zone can break up the Gravity by making every area of the space possess some.

- Placing one small object by itself tends to repel audiences unless it's very obviously intended for their use. This is because it might appear to be a focal point of action.

- The exact same layout can have totally different effects depending on where the audience enter from. Look at the example below:

- The audience entering from door A will emerge amidst the objects. This will create a Zone with heavy Gravity dispersed throughout, leading to a feeling of ease and a mobile audience.

- The audience entering from B will be confronted with an empty space with what looks like a stage full of scenery at the other end. They will not want to approach it without good reason.

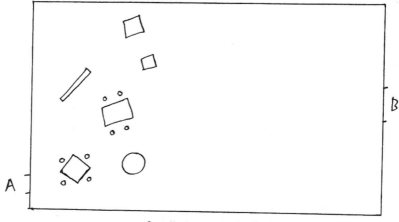

EFFECT OF ENTRANCES AND GRAVITY

Experiment with your layouts, even at the paper-sketching phase. You'll swiftly find yourself becoming quite adept at predicting how audiences will flow around a space.

Light Boundaries

An interesting thing happens when you start getting creative with lighting in an immersive piece.

When I directed *Loveplay*, we had a large room, pitch black except for one wide spotlight illuminating an area off to one side. Where, in this otherwise featureless Zone, do you think the audience congregated? I asked this question of a number of artists I work with, and all of them gave me one of three different answers. Some of them said they would congregate in the light, because it would feel more comfortable than being in darkness. A smaller number (mainly artists I've worked with on immersive projects) said they'd be spaced around the dark area, because the audience tends not to move into the focal point of the Zone. A couple of clever types, trying to catch me out, suggested they'd crowd around the walls regardless of where the light was.

I tried not to take pleasure in telling all three groups they were wrong.

Interestingly, the audience clustered on the edges of the lit area. Walls and Physical Boundaries became irrelevant, and this Light Boundary redefined the space totally. A ring of audience formed in the hazy area where the light and dark met. Just to test this, on another evening I lit the whole room equally. Once more, the Physical Boundaries reasserted themselves and the audience took their places around the walls.

Light is a powerful tool that can be used for more than just mood and aesthetics. The options at your disposal are beyond counting, and they don't rely on having a powerful lighting rig. You can achieve these effects with torches, bike lights and standing lanterns. One (slightly cheap) tactic is to use lights to trick the audience into ignoring the Physical Boundaries. The audience can enter a dark space with lanterns scattered around it. Once they've gravitated to the lights, a cast member can turn the main lights on; the audience are far more likely to stay where they are, even if that finds them in the middle of a large Zone. This technique can be used early on in, for example, the entrance procedure. Remember, you're always teaching your audience how to interact with your piece, so placing them in the middle of a Zone early on will help you achieve your vision.

One other thing to consider with lights is their colour. People gravitate towards natural light over unnatural, and white light over coloured. If you have the luxury of varied lighting, do your piece the honour of making the lights an integral part of your immersion.

Action Boundaries

Another principal tactic in your arsenal is to create Action Boundaries – this simply means using your cast to create the same effects that we've discussed with the lights and space. This is a concept that I've seen used to varying levels of success in most immersive pieces, and it goes hand in hand with our idea of Elegance. There is a very heavy-handed way to do this, by having cast members giving overt instructions and telling the audience where to go. This will probably work, but it immediately shatters the illusion of choice and freedom that you may be trying to create for the audience. If we wish to retain Elegance, creating Action Boundaries can be far more subtly done.

Your cast are your most powerful tool in the quest to keep your audience engaged. Unlike the set and lights, they can move and speak. Most importantly, they can also adapt to different situations. They can identify when the audience are reluctant to get involved and they can pinpoint which individuals might need more encouragement. With a tool that useful, it can be tempting just to assume that a company of actors will automatically sort those issues out on the night with a bit of minimal preparation. Nothing could be further from the truth, and the cast's role in this kind of interaction needs to be carefully workshopped and planned.

Rather than trying to squeeze this idea in a chapter to do with space, Chapter 3: Living Choices deals with all the possibilities here.

Using Different Boundaries Together

I presented the three types of Boundary in a specific order, and I suggest you address them in that way for your production. By having the Physical Boundaries largely worked out ahead of rehearsals (certainly by knowing the impact of the building's structure even if the actual design work isn't yet done), you then have a solid framework on which to consider Light and Action Boundaries.

In most cases, Physical and Light Boundaries exert a more constant influence on an audience than Action Boundaries; it would, therefore, be a mistake to use Action Boundaries (the actions of the cast) to try to overwhelm the effects of a Physical Boundary. Our #*MSND* case study showed this in practice, when the encouragement and dancing of the cast failed to overwhelm the Gravity of the space itself.

The only exception to this rule is when a cast member gives a specific instruction to the audience. Generally, the audience will obey this instruction but it *will not change their instincts*. Instructing the audience to dance in #*MSND* may have momentarily dragged people away from the walls, but the Physical Boundaries would have taken back control the minute that instruction was fulfilled.

Forcing the Void

After all the noise about making sure Voids never happen, I'm now going to tell you how to create them. Madness, you may cry. Not only have I told you we should avoid them, but surely if you wanted to create one anyway you would ignore everything I've already written? Well, not quite. But let's tackle these two questions in order.

Why would you intentionally create a Void? It can be an effective way of slowing the piece down. It can create tension. It can mould a vigorous and active mob into a compliant group more prone to fear. It can also be a barrier to exploration, which will be explained further when we discuss moving between rooms. For now, simply be aware that there may be times when you want to slow the audience down or create tension. There are a whole host of ways that an intentional Void can help you, but it must be used sparingly. We've already shown that it's hard work to galvanise an audience; anything that slows them down and discourages exploration will need to be thoroughly earned, or you'll be creating problems for yourself further down the line.

The bigger problem is about how to create a Void in the first place. Remember, a Void does not exist until the audience itself creates it. A huge, cold and empty aircraft hangar does not become a Void until an audience allows it to drag them to the walls. Earlier, we worked to reduce the probability of the Void forming. Now we need to increase this possibility. We call this process Forcing the Void.

The first step remains the same as Smashing the Void. Identify your Zones and look for places where a Void is already a possibility. You're simply not going to create a Void in a tiny storage cupboard, as the conditions will never be vast enough for even a solo audience member (you can create fear through claustrophobia in this environment, but that's a very different process to a Void). Once you've decided on where your Void could be created, you can begin playing with elements that encourage the audience's natural tendency to find the Boundaries. Use the tactics we've already discussed to create reverse effects. For example:

- Having furniture clustered mainly around the walls of the space, with a very clearly empty interior, will enhance the sense that the walls are the audience's 'home'.

- Place a single object in the centre of the space that looks like an incredibly important point of action for the play. Be careful to ensure that it doesn't break up the Zone into two separate ones. If the object is too large for the Void you're forcing, then it'll create comfort and smash the Void instead. For example, a small and lonely chair in the middle of our #MSND space may have forced the Void even though a podium in the same place smashed it.

- Use the first impression of the space to overwhelm the audience. Allow them to emerge into the emptiest part of the Zone, so that the first people to arrive are encouraged to walk along the walls rather than stride out into a large area. This will then make it even more likely that audience members behind them will follow, as they will be under the pressure of both the space's layout *and* the social pressure of conforming to the behaviour already occurring.

- Reinforce the static nature of traditional theatre. Place set pieces and furniture on the other side of the Zone from the audience to make them feel like they're walking into an auditorium. An armchair on the other side of the space will create a feeling that it's an area for the characters, not the audience.

LIVING SPACES

- Placing stronger lighting at the edges of the space will bring the Light and Physical Boundaries into cohesion, doubling their Gravity.

- A truly drastic measure is to have a physical barrier placed just inside the entrance. A desk or table directly in front of the door will bar people from walking directly forwards. Once they've started walking sideways, they'll tend to keep walking that way. This is a slightly un-Elegant solution as it's a bit obvious – but if you've been creating Elegance everywhere else you can get away with a bit of cheating!

The Funnel

Another special type of Zone is what I call a Funnel.

A Funnel is a Zone that keeps the audience moving and propels them through it. The perfect Funnel is a narrow corridor; the audience will continue moving until they find somewhere more comfortable to be. This idea of comfort (which we'll break down in a second) is at the heart of the Funnel, and complements the factors that create a Void. To create a Funnel, we combine at least two of three factors: Gravity, social pressure and claustrophobia. We've already discussed Gravity. The other two aren't new concepts we're creating, just well-known characteristics of human behaviour!

In this context, Gravity is something we can use to pull the audience through the space – and towards the object exerting the Gravity. Our other two factors do the opposite, pushing the audience away from certain situations.

First, Gravity. Imagine we have a narrow corridor, through which is moving a lone audience member (let's call her Lucy). There is every chance that Lucy could stop somewhere in the corridor. Assuming that nothing changes about the space and no other audience arrive, the decision to begin moving again is entirely in her hands. This may not be a problem most of the time, but we have decided that this corridor needs to be a Funnel. We want Lucy to be ejected swiftly out into the next Zone, where some climactic plot point will be resolved.

We can place an object at the end of the corridor, in Lucy's view, that exerts a Pull on her. Here, we're using Gravity to make entering another Zone seem attractive. This is a simple idea that I'm sure many of you would have come to by yourself. It's not, however, enough to make this Zone a Funnel. We're fairly certain that Lucy may begin ambling towards this interesting feature, arriving there in her own good time – hardly the sort of breakneck pace we're hoping for in this instance.

To increase that pace, we have a few options. Making that Gravity from the next space even more interesting is, of course, one way of doing this, but it still doesn't guarantee that Lucy will speed herself up. What we really need is a new kind of incentive, one that encourages her not just to explore the next Zone but to *leave* this Zone.

Before we do this, a side note: by using Gravity to drag Lucy from one Zone to the next, we're beginning to explore concepts called Flow and Pull, which we'll look at in far greater detail in the Journeys Through Space section of this chapter.

To encourage an audience to leave a space, we need to create a Push. A Push is an event or design feature that has the effect of making the audience want to leave an area (whereas a Pull encourages an audience to enter or remain in an area). We can create Push in many different ways, through both design and cast actions, but for now we're focusing on how we use space without the cast's influence. As I mentioned before, social pressure and claustrophobia are two of the most effective ways to create Push.

What does social pressure mean in this context? We've looked at it a little when we were exploring the formation of Voids (where fear of standing out is a key feature of our psychology in a group). When looking at Funnels, we're focused on a different aspect; generally an audience will avoid behaving in a way that ruins anyone else's experience. In any space, most audience members will move in such a way as to let others behind them pass through. If the space is confined in some way, such as in a narrow corridor, then sometimes the only option is to leave it entirely. This is obvious when a crowd moves through a corridor, but can be used to good effect elsewhere too. I've seen barriers put up in a large space that define a narrow path for the audience to move through; if you put action in the space outside the barriers, the audience are torn between their need to watch and the civilised impulse to let the people behind move along. You can use this technique to deposit people into the centre of a large space too; the placement of props or set pieces to either side of the entrance to a space can create a Funnel-like Zone that sends the audience into the centre of a space. This is one of the many ways that Funnels and Voids can work together, more on which later.

Claustrophobia is less to do with the layout of the space; it's more about how you use it. Imagine any Zone in your space. It can be a huge hangar or a small closet-like room. Fill it with audience until it's at least at a third capacity, then create the idea that they can't leave. Obviously, you probably can't lock them in, but you can certainly shut the door. You can post a surly-looking guard. Even a velvet rope hung across the entryway will create the effect. The second you remove that impediment, you have created a Funnel. The audience will get out of that Zone as quickly as possible, as you have placed the idea of imprisonment upon them. You need to be aware, however, that the barrier to leaving a space is not merely physical – it also exists in the audience's minds. You might open the door, but if they have been given an instruction to wait in this area then you haven't yet created a Funnel. Only by removing all restrictions simultaneously can this be achieved (in this example, you can do this simply by having whoever opens the door say 'Okay, off you go' as they open it).

These three ideas, combined, can create Funnels that propel the audience through them at breakneck speeds! Used in the right place, this can have quite breathtaking effects.

There are several reasons to use a Funnel, and how we go about creating it may be influenced by what effect we wish it to have. Below are some examples, but this is by no means an exhaustive list (if such a thing could even exist).

- After a tense and slow section of the performance, you might want to increase the pace of the audience's explorations. As we mentioned earlier, galvanising your audience into increased energy once they've slowed down is difficult, and a Funnel can help. Here, a social-pressure-fuelled Funnel can be incredibly helpful. Unlike Gravity and claustrophobia, social pressure is a Push based on other people's well-being – we may not respond to fear and we may choose not to explore the shiny object nearby, but generally people can be relied upon to be decent to each other.

- If you want to heighten tension, then a claustrophobia-fuelled Funnel could be perfect.

- We can impart a sense of wonder or fun by making the gravitational aspect of our Funnels more prominent. If there's a new discovery around every corner then our audience feels rewarded by moving through the space.

Combining Zones

The idea I'm about to present might be more appropriate in the next section, as it concerns journeys through multiple Zones, but I'm placing it here as it's the natural culmination of our work on different types of Zone.

When we start putting Funnels and Voids next to each other, we create effects that neither of these Zones can achieve by themselves. When we use either of these techniques, we're creating powerful thought patterns in the mind of an audience member. Combining different patterns and putting them in a sequence we choose means that we're creating an arc for these thoughts to go through. This is slightly abstract, but think of it this way:

We have all experienced joy. We have all experienced sadness. These two emotions are powerful, but when we combine them (such as uplifting the audience into joy after they have felt sadness) we begin to access other emotions that are only possible because of the *journey* between these two emotional states. We can create a joy coloured with relief, or a sadness tinted with frustration. In traditional forms of theatre, we do this all the time without having to discuss it in technical terms. Good theatre has always taken the audience on emotional journeys like these, and we're not doing anything new by exploring those dynamics.

There is one way, however, in which what we're doing *is* new; we're creating these experiences through our journeys in physical space. When we discuss emotional arcs created by the use of space, rather than the use of stories or characters, we need to understand exactly what is happening in the audience member. As human beings, we intuitively understand that an actor's speech or facial expressions can send us on emotional journeys. The vast majority of us are not used to discussing spaces explicitly as emotional factors.

Let me begin by describing an example. A 2014 production, *Montfort's March* (The Company, 2014, directed by Stephen Israel on Lewes South Downs National Park), managed to use Funnels and Voids effectively in an outdoor space. As the play reached its climactic scenes, the audience found themselves walking through narrow paths bounded by hedges, then by towering trees. Finally, the left-hand border of the Funnel was a cliff. Their pace picked up, and the sense of purpose was palpable. The last scene occurred at the top of a vast hill with an amazing view. It was the single best Void imaginable, and the audience were catapulted out into it from a series of Funnels. Their bewilderment was obvious, and the cast chose this moment to form them into ranks (as the scenario was a march towards a historic battle). The same dialogue delivered in a different space would have had far less effect, and was a stark lesson in the power of the space in an immersive production.

I'm going to assume that your production doesn't have access to a clifftop view over a historic battlefield. You can still form the same sorts of emotional arcs by using whatever Zones exist within your space, and once you break down this concept into simple questions, the process becomes quite straightforward. To do this, you need to already understand the Zones that you have in your space, so I'm assuming you've already done that work.

Work through this series of questions:

1. What emotional arc are you trying to create for the audience?

Answer this in as broad a way as possible. We're looking for answers like 'feeling positive, then having that feeling suddenly yanked away', or 'a feeling of danger, then becoming safe again'. By allowing a wide range of responses in these answers, you can maximise your chances of using the space you have rather than trying to fight against it (a topic we'll explore more fully in the next section, Features of the Space).

2. What Zones do you have in your space that can create that emotional arc?

Maybe you have a narrow corridor leading into a broad room (which can, of course, be used the other way round for a different arc). Maybe you have two huge rooms, but connected by a very small doorway that won't allow a huge flow of people through at once. Perhaps you have a glade of trees that opens into an open field.

3. When you place that broad emotional arc in these Zones, what new emotional journeys naturally emerge?

Let's say I was playing with the idea of 'a feeling of danger, then becoming safe again'. Each of the Zone combinations I proposed in question 2 would bring different nuances to that arc. The narrow corridor into the broad room lends itself to a feeling of being chased by something sinister before arriving in a safe haven. The two rooms linked by a small doorway can create the danger of not being able to get to safety in time, followed by the relief of emerging into a safe space. The forest leading into the field might evoke a sense of being hopelessly lost and isolated before arriving back in a recognisable location.

A mistake that can be made easily is to try to enforce a very defined emotional arc on a set of Zones that simply don't serve that purpose. Start broad, with the absolute necessities, then let your space do some of the work for you. With that in mind, this is the perfect time to start looking at the Features of the space.

Features of the Space

When you're considering your Zones, pay particular attention to their Features. Every room, every field and forest, every Zone will have them. They're the unique touches that make that space different to any other. They can be glaringly obvious, like a pillar in the middle of the room or a section of raised flooring. They may also be subtle, like the texturing on the walls or particularly interesting light fixtures. If you ignore these, you'll simultaneously underutilise the resources you've been given *and* make it more difficult to achieve your vision.

Most glaringly, you'll be missing pre-existing elements that can make your piece feel unique. This is relatively obvious; if there's a gnarled tree in the centre of the grove where you're performing, it'd be senseless not to incorporate this within your work. More subtly, though, there's the possibility you could start fighting against the space. I've seen a piece where the company tried to evoke a post-apocalyptic dystopia in a dishevelled but nicely decorated reception room. It didn't work. Not because it was the wrong space, but because they hadn't considered its inherent qualities. We were told we were in an underground vault, but not even the blacked-out windows could convince us that we were.

Let's imagine a scenario where we need to evoke that post-apocalyptic atmosphere in the particular space I mentioned above. There are two ways of doing this: Denying the Space or Incorporating the Space.

Denying the Space

Denying the Space means ignoring all the signals the space (and each Zone within it) is giving you. We take our well-appointed Georgian room and black out the windows. We play sound effects of creaking metal to evoke an industrial feel. Maybe we remove the furniture from the room and replace it with cold benches for the audience to sit on whilst they wait for the action to begin. We use fabric screens to block off areas from each other and create claustrophobia. We cover the walls with 1950s-style public-service announcements to enhance the feeling of a police state. Whatever we do, we use everything that we can to squash the inherent nature of the space and reshape it to our needs. We can never (unless we have a budget in the tens of thousands) totally deny the space's inbuilt properties, and if you *do* have that budget then why on earth have you chosen a space you have to reshape to this extent?

Incorporating the Space

If we Incorporate the Space, we take a different approach. We weigh up the Zones we have and the setting we wish to create. Our Zone, as we've said, is a comfortable but dilapidated reception room; our setting is that of an underground bunker in a post-apocalyptic dystopia. These two ideas are not immediately reconcilable, so we have to go deeper. Why do we want an underground bunker? What effect is it meant to achieve? There's two possible scenarios here that require different answers. One is that we are adapting a pre-existing play that is set within an underground bunker, and the other is that we are creating a new piece of work and we've decided a bunker is appropriate. Let's start by dealing with the issue of adapting a pre-existing piece of work.

In such a play, the bunker may be an integral part of the story. In Dennis Kelly's *After the End*, for example, it is a fundamental plot point that the piece takes place within the total isolation of an underground shelter. This is a useful play to use as a case study, so let's work with it. For those of you who've not encountered that play, it's a two-hander that takes place entirely in that setting. A major plot point is that the female character has been told that the world has ended by the male, but isn't certain whether he's telling the truth. Therefore, she cannot have any method of looking at the outside world if we're going to stay remotely true to the original plot.

Before we go any further and look at how to overcome these issues, bear in mind that you will be bound by any restrictions you agreed to when you acquired the rights to this play. Hopefully, if you've gained permission to adapt a non-immersive book or play into an immersive format, you will have a certain amount of freedom to adapt certain aspects, but check with the holder of the rights about specific aspects like adapting dialogue.

We have two options here. We can either decide that this piece and this space fundamentally can't function well together, and this is sometimes a valid choice. Hopefully, you will have been sufficiently careful in your early choices; I would hope that no one would want to stage a totally faithful adaptation of *After the End* in a field. Our other option is to start deconstructing the function of that underground setting in that play.

By interrogating the play, we discover that the bunker creates certain circumstances:

1. It prevents the female character from seeing the outside world for herself.

2. It creates the post-apocalyptic feeling required of the play.

3. It justifies certain lines of dialogue that refer to being in an underground bunker.

The first issue above is fundamental to the story. It's a hard line that can't be crossed without changing your production from *After the End* to *Inspired By After the End*! So how can we keep that circumstance whilst Incorporating the Space? One possible answer is to check if there are any windowless rooms within the building we're using, or a basement or attic. Can you make the play work with minimal changes whilst acknowledging that we're in a secure room rather than an underground bunker?

The second issue is the most easily remedied, and you can read the section after this one for more on how we create the tone we need whilst changing settings.

The third issue seems like the most easily solved; we can just change the lines of dialogue, right? Well, this is probably the hardest to do legally. Every production of every play has different rights attached to it, and it's very difficult to get permission to change the writer's words. I can't offer any general advice here, as resolving this aspect of the problem will rely on your communication with the rights holder.

When we're devising our own new work, it's admittedly a lot easier to work with the space than when we're taking a pre-existing text. Consider those two questions we asked about our setting: Why do we want an underground bunker? What effect is it meant to achieve?

Maybe we're looking to create the image of a refuge from danger, but one that is precarious and controlled by an authoritarian power. With that in mind, we start creating that refuge in our space.

Rather than blacking out the windows, we have soldiers warily peering out of them, looking for signs of danger. The early evening sunlight streaming through the windows taunts a cast that hasn't been able to go outside in some time. An exhausted colonel is wearily sunken into one of the space's threadbare armchairs, suspiciously eyeing the audience as they arrive. Military supplies are crammed in whatever niches and alcoves exist in the space, wedged between the now-inconvenient furniture already in the space. The receiving officer has brought the family's drinks cabinet over to the door, using it as a makeshift desk. He signs in the audience as they arrive and waves at them to find a space wherever they can. They find themselves constantly having to move as the soldiers try to go about their business in a building that was never designed for this amount of traffic (neatly dispelling any Voids that might occur).

By Incorporating the Space, a smaller amount of effort than you would spend creating a nuclear bunker can have many more pro-found effects. The scene we created above can put you in mind of the climactic scenes of *28 Days Later*, the acclaimed Danny Boyle movie about a zombie epidemic sweeping London. It's rarely a good choice to fight against your space; allow it to help you by honing in on what you want to achieve. It's tempting to become attached to the movie in our heads even when that movie isn't achievable. Be ruthless and decide what the basic aesthetic, emotional and intellectual thrust of the space should be, and what you can achieve within it. 'Faded grandeur' or 'bizarre and disturbing fantasy' are far more workable concepts than 'ruined palace' and 'disused carousel'!

Journeys Through Space

Giving your audience freedom of movement around the space requires you, obviously, to *know* your space in the first place. This section is built on the idea that you're using a multi-space venue, with various rooms and/or corridors. If you're using a traditional theatre or one large room, the bulk of this may not apply to you – but there are still useful tips for your piece.

First up, this is the second section in this Living Spaces chapter, but that doesn't mean this work all happens *after* the previous section, How to Use a Room. If you're using a multi-Zoned space, this work will be happening alongside and supporting the ideas we spoke about earlier.

Your first step is to create a ground plan of your performance space. Ideally, a proper technical blueprint can be obtained from the owners of the building, but failing that you can do just as well with a carefully hand-drawn map. If you go down this route, you *must* make sure to include notes about sightlines; I've seen more than a few problems arise in performance because companies ignored this. It's all very well to have the conspirators huddled in a corner while they experience a climactic part of the plot, but if someone two doors away can see them and ruin the secret meeting then it's all for naught.

Indicate where the audience enters from with a big clear arrow; when we come to talk about Flow (more on that later), you'll be surprised how something so obvious can make your life easier. Note down also if there are any easily accessible areas that you want to be off-limits to the audience at any point ('as few as possible' is my advice), and whether doorways between rooms have doors that can be opened or closed. Then there are the legal necessities of using a space; fire exits, considerations towards accessibility and other such factors can't be compromised on.

Finally, all this done, cast an eye over the blueprint and see if you can visualise where large groups of the audience might start congregating without being told to, and what rooms they're less likely to go to of their own free will. This is the beginning of imagining what I call the Flow of the space, and getting it right will possibly save your sanity.

The Basics: Flow and Hubs

The Flow of the space is a concise way of talking about how audiences are likely to move without any prodding from your company. Obviously, every audience is different, but you can draw basic conclusions and plan your production accordingly.

The first thing to understand is where your play's Hub (or Hubs) might be. A Hub is a Zone where audience members are likely to congregate, a sort of default safe haven for lost, nervous, tired or bored people. It is very likely that if you don't consciously define one, the audience will choose one for you – and it might be somewhere problematic. Keeping that choice in your hands means you can use it to your advantage later on, rather than being frustrated by a herd of bewildered theatregoers eating a sandwich in a room you really need to turn into a forest right now.

In addition to making sure the audience doesn't hinder the production by choosing an unhelpful Hub for themselves, creating your own will actively help you achieve your vision. As we go through this section and talk about Flow, Pull and Dividing, you'll come to see that having a Hub gives you a subtle but firm control over your production. Explaining *why* this is the case can only be done through explaining all of the concepts in this chapter, so for now, just trust me on this one!

You need to choose a Hub – and, more importantly, make the audience treat it as such. You could just tell them, sure, but I like to think we're all a little bit more creative and subtle than that. The better option is to figure out where the audience is likely to gravitate towards instinctively and use that to your advantage. This is likely to be the nearest space to the entrance that is large enough to hold a large number of the audience members comfortably, and contains relatively non-threatening interactions.

Let's imagine some scenarios then. Overleaf is a map of a space I used for a production.

Imagine you are using this space, but have a choice of entry points for the audience: the Great Hall (A), the Waiting Room (B) or the Cellar (C). Even without having visited the space, you can make a good guess as to where the first Hubs could emerge. Have a look, and try to identify likely Hubs from each of those entrances before reading any further. For reference, the Central Room in the centre is roughly the size of a large lounge or front room.

The Great Hall and Waiting Room would both, in all probability, act as their own Hubs. They're large spaces and as close to their entrances as they can get. As long as you didn't place a slavering monster intent on devouring them in the corner of the room, the audience would likely congregate there.

The Cellar is a trickier prospect. The entrance itself has a low ceiling, the next room is small, and the Pathway is a narrow corridor. Your first viable Hubs are likely to be either the Central Room or the Store Room. It would then be up to you to draw the audience into one or the other and make it feel like a safe space.

It's very possible for multiple Hubs to arise in a production. If my audience came from the Waiting Room, using it as their Hub, I could make events happen in the Great Hall that would shift the centre of focus there – but the audience will always need a big incentive to move from somewhere that's proved itself safe and friendly. Now, just to be clear, I'm not saying that the audience won't leave the Hub... I'm saying that, in a totally free-roaming piece, it will be the place they

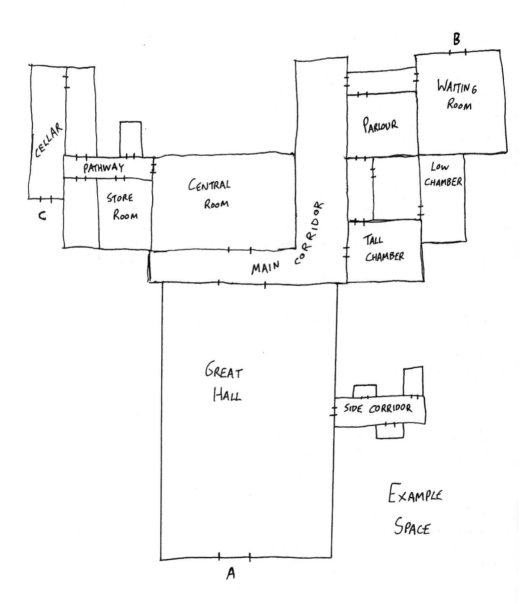

CELLAR

C

PATHWAY

STORE
ROOM

CENTRAL
ROOM

MAIN CORRIDOR

PARLOUR

TALL
CHAMBER

B

WAITING
ROOM

LOW
CHAMBER

GREAT
HALL

SIDE CORRIDOR

EXAMPLE
SPACE

A

48

tend to return to. When they're confused, fearful, tired or want to socialise (if that's appropriate to your piece), this is where they'll come back to.

A useful analogy would be to imagine that all audience members are attached by elastic to the Hub. Different audience members will have different lengths and strengths of elastic, but it will generally tug them back to their Hub now and then. When you plan something truly exciting to happen away from your Hub, you need to have ensured you've given enough incentive to explore that far in the first place.

Your job now is to identify the likely initial Hub in your space. Moving forwards, we'll look at how to use it to your advantage.

Pull

Knowing where your Hub is, you can work outwards to establish the Pull of different Zones of your space. Pull is the next aspect of Flow, and is how we describe the ease of getting the audience to spend time in a certain area. If a room has high Pull, the audience will probably gravitate towards it of their own accord. If it has low Pull, they won't. Understanding the Pull in your space allows you to plan how and when you need to encourage your audience to explore further afield. Getting this right can be the difference between a truly Elegant piece or awkwardly telling the audience where they can and can't go.

Working out Pull is useful because it allows us to tie together the progress of the story and the audience's physical journey. When we know the Pull of various different Zones, we can place important scenes in well-travelled rooms, and secrets in hidden nooks.

Pull isn't an exact equation or science, but is relatively easy to work out. The space with the highest Pull will be the Hub, for all the reasons we've already discussed (that is, in fact, the very thing that makes it the Hub). Pull will decrease according to various factors. Generally, an area's Pull will depend on these criteria:

1. The distance from the Hub.

2. The comfort and size of the Zone.

3. How visually interesting the Zone is.

4. The number of rewarding experiences occurring within that Zone.

5. How easy it is to detect new experiences happening within that Zone from elsewhere in the space.

6. The Pull of the Zones between the Hub and the Zone you're considering (which, combined, tell us the Pull of the entire journey between them).

As we talk about each of these ideas, refer back to your ground plan; it's easier to talk about these ideas if we apply them rather than making this dry and theoretical. What we're about to lay out here are basic, average factors. You will *almost always* have audience members who are less affected by certain conditions. Some will explore further, others will seek experience over comfort... But the baseline group behaviour will likely stick to these ideas pretty closely.

1. Distance

The first factor is easy to work out. The further the audience have to move from the Hub, the fewer of them will make it there. Referring back to our map, then, have a quick look at where the furthest spaces are from each entrance. From the Great Hall, the farthest journeys are to the Cellar and the Waiting Room. The Waiting Room's farthest journeys are to the Cellar and the Side Corridor, whilst if we start at the Cellar our furthest journey is to the Waiting Room and the Side Corridor.

Just from considering this first idea, then, you can see that choosing a different entrance will drastically alter how your space is used. The Parlour would be frequently reached from the Waiting Room, but very off the beaten track from the other two choices of entrance. This obviously impacts what action you place there.

2. Comfort and Size

The audience is unlikely to stand and wait in a tiny cramped closet. Big open spaces hold the subconscious promise that something will *happen* here. Because of this, bigger spaces (and, to a lesser extent, more comfortable spaces) have greater Pull than small cramped ones. For example, look at the Store Room; this space will have greater Pull than the small unnamed room directly to the north. The audience can congregate there without feeling claustrophobic, and it seems far more likely that something will occur there.

When looking at the size of the room, you'll probably end up considering its Void potential. This makes up part of point 4, Rewarding Experiences, slightly further on in this list.

3. Visual Interest

This is probably the least powerful influence on Pull, but it does have an impact. Imagine it like this: there are two almost identical rooms, equidistant from the Hub. The only difference between them is that one has a throne in it... Or a chandelier, or a statue, or a locked box. All other things being equal, that object of interest will give the room more Pull than its drabber sibling.

Crucially, though, this will only increase the zone's Pull *after the audience has already been there*. As we'll consider later, Pull can be changed throughout the production. Where this becomes interesting is that it's the first factor you can directly influence. You can't move rooms around, but you *can* put something of interest in a room. This has all sorts of possibilities that we'll explore later when we talk about using Flow to your advantage.

4. Rewarding Experiences

If the audience is rewarded for finding a certain space (for example, by overhearing a secret conversation between characters that gives them insight into the plot), they'll want to come back there again.

This is a powerful tool, as it's another way you can change the Pull of a space mid-performance. At its furthest extent, this is one of the ways you can make the audience choose a new Hub – from the Waiting Room to the Great Hall, for example.

5. Ease of Detection

This is a big tool at your disposal, potentially the most powerful way of making the audience go where you want. Imagine this scenario:

You're running the same play, but one night the audience starts in the Great Hall and on another night they start in the Waiting Room. You decide that the first major event is a scene that occurs in the nearest medium-sized space to the entrance (that isn't the entrance itself). From the Great Hall, that's the Central Room; from the Waiting Room, it's the Parlour. Both these rooms are equidistant from their Hubs, and have similar journeys. You leave the Hub, cross a short corridor, and arrive in the new room. So if I were to say that the Central Room would have *much* more Pull than the Parlour, why might that be?

The answer is in the sightlines. From the Great Hall, you can both see and hear things occurring in the Central Room, whilst from the Waiting Room you might be able to hear the next scene but you won't see it. By giving the audience greater incentives to explore (in the form of proof that events are taking place in another room), you increase the Pull of that room. Looking at our map, you can see sightlines that will increase Pull in quite distant spaces. There's a direct line of sight from the corridor next to the Waiting Room all the way through the Parlour to the Tall Chamber. If you were starting from the Waiting Room, that's going to give the Tall Chamber a hell of a lot more Pull than the Central Room, even though it isn't much closer to the Entrance.

You can even make the audience ignore *closer* spaces with this technique. Imagine your play starts in the Cellar. The audience have found their way to the Pathway, and you don't really want them going in the room just to the south quite yet. So you place a scene by the top wall of the Central Room, using that sightline to draw the audience towards that action. When I mentioned Pull being a tool that allows your piece to be Elegant, this is partly what I meant. You don't need to place a guard by the door forbidding your audience entry into the room off the Pathway if you use the Pull in this way.

6. The Journey There

Spaces don't exist in isolation. To get from the Great Hall to the Low Chamber, the audience need to go through the Main Corridor and the Tall Chamber – and that means you have to consider the Pull of each step in the journey to the destination. It's useless to make that final room the most Pull-exerting space in the play if it's hidden behind a labyrinth of uninteresting and Pull-less spaces. This means that making a distant space have the same Pull as a nearer space is a harder task, and you should plan your piece accordingly.

This is a rabbit hole that can totally consume you if you're not careful! If we were really to hone in on the Pull of the space across the length of the play, then we would find that every Zone was in a constant state of flux. The Pull would be increasing and decreasing at all times, and at different rates for different audience members. It is totally impractical to plan for every single permutation of Pull, which is one of the reasons that establishing your Hub early in the production is so useful. Periodic returns to the Hub can 'reset' an audience member's relationship to the space, reasserting the basic Pull strengths you've worked out in advance. Using factors like rewarding experiences and visual interest will still shift the audience's perceptions over the course of the performance, but other factors (such as distance) remain constant.

Working Out Pull

Now you should be able to look at your own space and consider the Pull. Work outwards from your Hub, figuring out where the hidden nooks and crannies in your space are.

One last point about Pull before we move on: you don't necessarily want every Zone to have a lot of Pull. It can be very rewarding to have areas that are more hidden and secretive. We'll talk more about that later.

Regions

When you're working with a large space like the one in our example, the idea of Regions can help. Regions are multi-Zone areas in your space that link together and feed off each other. For example, the Side Corridor heading east from the Great Hall has lots of little rooms jutting from it. This is a Region; someone in one part of that Region is likely to encounter other things happening in that Region.

Defining a Region is a nebulous thing, with no hard rules, but most of the ideas around Pull will work for Regions too. In our example, the way Regions work can also be affected by which entrance you choose. You can also use broad brushstrokes, choosing just a couple of large Regions, or get very specific, with many interlocking and overlapping small Regions. How much detail to go into should depend on the complexity of your production.

Sometimes Regions overlap. The Great Hall and the Central Room could be considered part of the same Region; they're nearby, and the audience can see directly from one into the another. The Central Room and the Pathway are also definitely part of a Region together, but the Pathway and the Great Hall are not.

Let's work out what Regions there are in our ground plan on page 48. Come up with your own ideas and note them down before reading further. For the sake of simplicity, let's assume our immersive production starts in the Great Hall. It's best not to get too obsessive over defining Regions, and better to end up with a few useful Regions rather than twenty-five different overlapping ones.

I'm going to break the ground plan down into six broad Regions – I could go more granular if the piece required it, but this is enough to illustrate the concept. These are:

1. The Great Hall and the Central Room.

2. The Side Corridor and its offshoot rooms (possibly including the Great Hall depending on how much visible action occurs in the corridor itself).

3. The Central Room, the Pathway, the Store Room and the unnamed chamber above the Pathway.

4. The Cellar, the western end of the Pathway and the two narrow chambers jutting off from the western end of the Pathway.

5. The Tall Chamber, the Parlour and the Low Chamber.

6. The Waiting Room, the Parlour, the north end of the main corridor and the small east-west corridor above the Parlour.

Regions tend to exert a hold on audiences. Whilst you will have people who wander merrily from room to room without much purpose, people tend to want to explore the area they've arrived in. Let's look at an example.

On their first explorations, someone has moved from the Great Hall to the Central Room. Now, to their left, they see a new corridor opening up (which you and I know will lead them into a new Region), taking them deeper on the path they've chosen. All other things being equal, the majority of the audience are not likely to turn on their heel and go to the Tall Chamber instead.

You can use Regions to your advantage, especially combined with Pull. Let's say we want the audience, starting in the Great Hall, to see an event in the Store Room early on in the production. They might head in that direction, but equally they might head off down the Main Corridor past the Tall Chamber, towards the Waiting Room. How do we get as much of the audience as possible going in the 'right' direction whilst keeping this Elegant?

Well, we know the Central Room has a lot of Pull, and we know the Central Room shares a Region with the Store Room. So one possible solution would be to ramp up the Central Room's Pull even further.

As the first audience members start leaving the Great Hall, a cast member in the Central Room looks startled by them and darts off towards the Pathway. We've just added an interaction to the Central Room to increase its Pull (we've also increased the Pull of the Zones further on, where the cast member fled to). Just to be really certain, we also make the lighting in the Central Room a garish pink and have cushions scattered around it, making it more attractive than the corridor they might otherwise take. Most of them head in that direction. Note that we've added so much Pull to this room that most of the audience will follow; if you want to attract only a portion of the audience, there's techniques later in this chapter that will help.

At that point, we trust in the power of the Region to keep most of them heading in that direction. They'll pass the Store Room and see what's going on there. We've directed the audience where we want them to go without either removing or overtly discouraging their ability to choose otherwise. You will, of course, get the occasional adventurous soul actively resisting the Flow of the Regions and heading back in the opposite direction; never assume that Flow controls your audience. The best we can do is to *influence* them.

Managing Flow

Everything we've been talking about so far has been based on this idea of Flow; that every space has a natural Push and Pull of its own that will subtly influence the audience. We've explored a little of how you work with the Flow of a space, but let's talk now about planning your piece to make the most of it.

Your production is almost certainly going to have a Hub, and you know now that you should take control of where that space is. Hopefully by now you're starting to understand why. The Pull of each room is related to the Hub the audience is starting from, so taking control of that first decision means you have a basis for planning your piece. How you create the Hub is up to you, and should be something that resonates well with your piece's plot and theme. It might be the bar where the gangsters are hanging out, the processing chamber for the nuclear bunker your audience have been granted access to, or the waiting room at the station for their grand journey on the Orient Express.

When you establish the Hub, you have the opportunity to set the level of free-roaming behaviour you expect from the audience. It's important to do this early, because it is *very* difficult to make an audience change its behaviour once it's established. There are many different behaviours you can encourage when creating the Hub, but I'll give you two opposite examples as a starting point.

A Structured Experience

'This is a relatively structured immersive experience, and I want the audience to move around but not just explore aimlessly. They might miss bits of the story!'

If this is how you want your piece to operate, your Hub should be a room filled with interactions – and these interactions should be relatively non-hostile. Now, depending on the tone of your piece, that doesn't necessarily mean handing out hugs and lollipops. If your play is set in a gritty post-apocalyptic dystopia, your grim-faced soldiers may well be thoroughly unpleasant. The important point is whether the Hub is a better place to remain than the unknown outside the room. Cold-eyed killer soldiers and cold metal benches are fine if the outside world is a nuclear wasteland populated by flesh-eating mutants, but not if the outside world is a cosy suburban neighbourhood!

Having some sort of 'scene' in the Hub is crucial. Giving the audience a shared experience right from the start will cement the feeling of being in a group. Once they leave the Hub to start exploring, they will tend to move in a more herd-based way. They'll also tend to follow trailblazers – once four or five people go in a certain direction, the rest are likely to follow their lead.

The advantage of this approach is that it requires less planning. Let's take our example ground plan and start in the Waiting Room. With the kind of opening Hub-based experience I've just described, we're

LIVING SPACES

then free to plan a storyline that moves roughly from that Hub, down the Main Corridor to the Central Room, through to the Cellar, then back to the Great Hall for the conclusion of the piece. Because you've created a more structured movement pattern, you don't have to put as much planning in the unused rooms as you otherwise would. When the audience is heading to the Central Room at the start, you can put something mildly interesting in the Great Hall, but the story is clearly moving into the Central Room. You probably don't need to put any significant action in the Side Corridor at that point, because the nature of the play has made it clear where the audience will find their greatest Rewards; audience members are unlikely to venture so far off the beaten track into this Region. However, once they reach the Great Hall near the end of the performance, attention needs to be paid to the Side Corridor... but you'll have long since stopped putting action in the Waiting Room.

You will still have to plan a little more than if you were doing a set guided tour though... From the Waiting Room, our audience may choose to head through the Low Chamber, eventually emerging through the Tall Chamber. The direction of travel remains the same, but both routes should involve some level of Reward. There is a fine line between encouraging the audience to follow the story and punishing them for wanting to explore your world.

The drawbacks to this approach are worth considering though. Firstly, if you do get a more adventurous audience member who veers off in other directions, you may leave them feeling a little railroaded when their personal forays end without satisfaction.

Far more problematic though, is that you will be training your audience to be quite compliant. Changing this behaviour will be difficult, so if you do want them to act on their own initiative at any point you'll be working damn hard to make it happen. Every time you Reward an audience member for following the pack, you make *not* following the pack an increasingly unattractive option. This will not only affect how and where they move; it will spill over into how they interact with the cast and the performance.

An Exploratory Experience

'Right from the start, I want my audience to explore, to go where they want. I'd hate it if they waited to be told what to do.'

If you want to enable the audience to take charge of their own journey, how you control the Hub at the start is incredibly important. You need to establish the Hub's status as a safe space, but you also need to create the desire for your audience to go outside it voluntarily. The biggest mistake you can make here is to start the play with a static scene in the Hub. That would cement, instantly, the idea that the play will come to the audience as opposed to them going out and discovering it for themselves.

Use your Regions effectively, and make it clear that action is always happening elsewhere. From the Great Hall, for instance, present action in the Central Room to encourage them to leave. Then have audible action happening at the same time in the Tall Chamber so that upon leaving the Hub, they're presented with a choice of routes. From the Waiting Room, present action in the Low Chamber whilst simultaneously having characters heading out of the corridor to the west. Meanwhile, starting at the Cellar will send your audience to the Pathway anyway, so make sure there's action in the Central Room and the Store Room. As the Store Room is a dead end, make the action in there something that Rewards staying in place for a short time rather than just being a stopgap on the way to the Central Room. Encouraging static behaviour may sound contradictory to creating a free-roaming audience, but in this case we're enforcing a choice upon the audience of which action to witness. Every Zone needs to both draw the audience towards it and make it difficult to leave. If every Zone is fulfilling these purposes, this will create a fragmented audience exploring according to their tastes.

It also makes sense to have the 'main storyline' dispersed amongst different spaces. If you have three different options on the audience's path but one of them is patently the one that they need to see in order to understand the story, then you've undone a lot of your hard work. If there are a few essential scenes you need the audience to witness, then the techniques you've learned in this chapter can be used to draw them there without undermining the idea of a free-roaming production.

Dividing the Audience

We've talked at length about how to get the audience to go where you want them to go whilst preserving their freedom. However, in a free-roaming performance, you often want the audience to divide and explore in different directions. This presents a difficulty; when everyone is being presented with the same amounts of Pull, how do you get them heading off on their own individual path?

There are three basic ways of doing this using Pull, and I group them all under the category of Dividing the Audience. There is also a way of doing this without using Pull, which I'll talk about last.

1. Splitting the Audience

Splitting is a way of getting the audience to break off into multiple groups of roughly equal size. You do this by highlighting two options of equal Pull to the audience. By making two events happen simultaneously, and making them time-limited events (so the audience can only see one), you will Divide the audience *and* teach them that they cannot see everything in this piece.

This process can be repeated multiple times across the production; having split an audience into two segments, you can then further split each of these two segments with additional Splitting choices. You can also split the audience into more than two groups, but it can be very difficult to create three or more areas of equal Pull – especially if you're working in a smaller space.

As I mentioned earlier, you cannot control what an *individual* audience member does. We can predict that a roughly equal section of the audience may explore each option in a split, but not which person will explore which option. This isn't immediately a problem, but if you create further splits later in the production it can become relevant.

Imagine you have created a simple two-way split, creating two different segments of audience who have different experiences. Later, they have merged back into one group at the Hub. You decide you want to split them once again, to allow them to experience developments to the events they witnessed earlier. You will need to bear in mind that you will *never* recreate the exact same segments again – this later split will almost certainly create different groups to the earlier split. This means that enjoying the scenes you present in a later split cannot rely upon having seen a particular branch of an earlier split.

Simply put, in an audience of fifty people, the chance of organically recreating the exact same two segments in a later split is 1:1,125,899,906,842,624. Admittedly, this number does assume that the audience's choice is entirely random and we can influence the audience's choices through many methods... But it would be far easier not to rely on them making the choice you need them to make!

Splitting is especially useful early on in your piece. If, despite your best efforts, your audience has shuffled in a zombie-like horde, Splitting will help create a more dynamic production.

2. Shaving the Audience

Shaving is a way of using the more adventurous members of the audience, exploiting their tendency to wander further afield for your own ends.

Sometimes, you may not want an area to be discovered by everybody, or even by a large number of the audience. This might be because you want to turn the audience against each other in Factions, or because secrecy and conspiracy is part of your theme... But whatever your reason, Shaving is how you can create an 'elite' mini-group of audience.

The idea is similar to Splitting, in that you create two or more simultaneous opportunities for the audience. However, one of those opportunities will have less Pull than the other. A smaller number will explore this less obvious possibility, Shaving them off from the larger mass of audience.

This is actually more difficult to manage correctly than it sounds, mainly because you can't predict how many people will explore this lower Pull event. It may be that, during one performance, no one explores it. On another night, a particularly adventurous audience may head towards it in droves (though this will still sort of do the job, because then the higher Pull event will shave off some audience). Because of these variables, you need to plan carefully what goes on in that lower Pull room and to judge quite what its Pull should be.

First, consider the event that will be used to shave off this audience segment. It can't be something throwaway or unimportant, because that would punish your audience for exploring. Equally, it can't be something so important that the plot can't function without audience seeing it, because it may go unwatched. My personal tactic is normally to use Shaving scenes to give background, secrets or character motivations to the main plot. Whatever you choose, you need to make sure the experience is rewarding and dramatically rich, but can be missed.

For our second consideration, exactly how much Pull to give it, you need to consider how finely you want to shave the audience. Maybe you want, at most, just one or two people to find their way to it – or maybe you want a good third of the audience to head that direction. The size of that audience segment will dictate what Pull you give it.

To decide the appropriate level of Pull, you're going to walk a tightrope between two extremes. It must have less Pull than the 'main' scene to which you're sending the majority of the audience. However, it must also have *more* Pull than the other, irrelevant Zones in the space (which I call Background Pull). Remember, all Zones have a level of Pull at all times, not just when you're thinking about them.

If your Shaving scene has only slightly less Pull than the main scene (for example, the main scene is in the Great Hall and the audience can see the Shaving scene is in the Central Room), it'll draw the attention of a significant chunk of the audience (possibly to the point where this becomes a Split rather than a Shave). On the other hand, if it's no greater than the rest of the space (the main scene is in the Great Hall, the shave scene in the Low Chamber with no clues to its existence), only hardened explorers will find it. A middle ground between these extremes might be to have the main scene in the Great Hall with an event happening in the Tall Chamber that can be heard from the northern half of the Great Hall.

Shaving's a difficult thing to pin down, and you should never use it to dictate a specific requirement such as 'exactly seven audience members should see this scene'. It's simply not something you can control. But it does have one advantage we haven't yet talked about...

The audience will do your work for you. Finding a Shaving scene will *excite* them, and they will tell other people about their discovery. Having your audience teach each other to explore is a Holy Grail in this kind of piece, and it's something you'll thank yourself for setting up. Bear in mind that Shaving can be combined with Splitting in the same moment. Presenting three choices, where one has significantly less Pull than the other two (which are roughly equal to each other in their Pull), will shave a small segment of the audience and split the remaining segment.

3. Dispersing the Audience

Use Dispersing sparingly because, frankly, it's a bit cheap... But sometimes cheap works. This is a technique that works best later in the production, when the audience have had a chance to get to know the space.

Dispersing is a way of splintering the audience into small fragments, and sending those fragments wandering around the space. It's a useful tactic if you've just had a big, long scene that keeps the audience in one room for an extended time, and it's relatively simple to achieve. It's best used in a space that has more than one exit, as that immediately breaks up the audience rather than having a herd leave through one door.

To disperse, you create a stimulus to leave the current space. It could be as heavy-handed as guards clearing the room, or as simple as the priest thanking the congregation and informing them the mass is over. You then have to ensure that there are no immediately obvious scenes in the surrounding rooms. The idea is that the audience has to choose a route to explore *before* they see a scene in progress. For example, you want to disperse the Great Hall; you cannot have scenes occurring in the Side Corridor, the Central Room or the Tall Chamber, because these would automatically exert their Pull and draw the audience towards them in a group.

Instead, you'd put scenes in the Store Room, the Low Chamber, the Waiting Room and the Toilet itself. Each of these will only be found by audience members having chosen (at random) to explore in that direction.

Now, I referred to this tactic as cheap, and if you overuse it you could leave the audience feeling like the space is empty and unplanned rather than giving them the sensation of hunting for the story. You can alleviate this by having minor events scattered along the routes through the space. These could be, for example, a character smoking a stage cigarette in the corner of the Main Corridor; two characters speaking in hushed tones in the Pathway who scatter nervously when they see any audience members; someone asking for loose change in the Tall Chamber...

When Dispersing, you're using the opposite of Pull. Rather than having a scene Pull the audience towards itself, you instead Push them away from their starting point. By using minor events to continue Pushing them onwards (making it clear that, yes, there are experiences to be discovered in this direction), and by making sure there are enough endpoints they can find with significant scenes, Dispersing can get your audience spread throughout the space. You also might want to consider what happens if your audience is Dispersed and finds themselves in a Void or Funnel...

4. Extracting the Audience

I mentioned a fourth method of Dividing the audience that doesn't use the qualities of the space. This method, Extracting the Audience, doesn't truly sit within the techniques we've explored in this chapter, but since we're talking about ways of Dividing the audience I've elected to place it here. Chapter 3: Living Choices features a more in-depth discussion of Extracting the Audience.

This method involves getting cast members to send audiences in certain directions. This can be done in a number of ways, with varying degrees of complexity and randomness. The cast can select an audience member or group and lead them to an otherwise hidden scene, giving the cast the ability to actively choose how to Divide the audience. One production I heard of had playing cards distributed at random amongst the audience, with people holding a certain suit of card being led in a certain direction.

These can be effective when used well, but they lead to significantly different effects on the audience's psychology. Most immediately, these techniques give no element of proactive decision-making to the audience member. Their destination has been chosen in advance, either by a cast member or by random chance. If you're looking to create a free-roaming and independent audience, these techniques don't enhance that mindset.

You also have to be careful about how to maintain Elegance in these circumstances. If playing cards are an inappropriate choice for your production, it's not simply a matter of choosing a more aesthetically relevant object ('We'll use golden tickets instead!'); there are deeper questions to ask. Does the distribution of random objects feel in-keeping with the world you're creating for your audience, or is it an obvious logistical tactic? Are you straining the audience's immersion in your world?

The style of performance you're presenting will have an impact on the suitability of these methods. If your goal is to have the audience feel like characters within this world, then they may be a step too far away from Elegance. However, many productions don't have this aim; a Punchdrunk-style piece of Exploration Theatre can use these more comfortably as the experience doesn't necessarily rely on the audiences's wholesale immersion into their 'character'.

Other Considerations

When we're planning how to use these methods, it can be easy to forget that audience members have memories and that their experiences will shape their future decisions. This has a number of effects that will grow in intensity during any single run of the production.

Most immediately, it will affect their decision-making when you're using any of these Dividing tactics. When the audience enters the space for the first time, they come in as relatively blank slates. They will respond to the techniques presented in this chapter in a way that is largely predictable. There are some conditions to this; three audience members who come to the production as a group are more likely to follow each other than split, for example.

Once the audience has experienced some choices and interactions, their behaviour will begin to change in ways that you may not have planned. For instance, a group of audience members who were shaved together may start to develop a sort of pack mentality, making it more likely that they will stick together even if they were strangers to each other before the production commenced. This is a very exciting opportunity if you incorporate it into your plans, as you can take advantage of these new loyalties, using them to present the audience with difficult choices (see the section on Factions in Chapter 3: Living Choices for more on this). The drawback, though, is that Dividing tactics become less reliable as the production progresses. These personal relationships (along with many other factors, such as whether someone has had an enjoyable experience in a certain Zone previously) begin to exert their own social Pull that competes with the spatial Pull you've created. You may create a moment that seems perfectly designed to create a clean split in the audience, only to find that you forgot to account for previous events that turn it into a pronounced shave.

In isolation, these unexpected results shouldn't be a significant problem, but if you've set up complex chains of splits and shaves then the knock-on effects can grow larger and larger until they derail the production. You can absolutely plan your production to take advantage of all these psychological factors, with the obvious consequence that your preparation will grow in scale by a huge amount. A simpler way to limit the effects is to reduce how many elements of your production *rely* upon your predictions being correct. If the fifth moment of interaction in the play depends upon the first four proceeding exactly according to your predictions, you're creating potential problems for yourself further down the line.

Leaving the Space

With care and planning, your space can be so much more than just a series of rooms. Explore the potential within each room, and the opportunities presented by the journeys between them – your piece can only benefit from this vast, unexpected cast member. No other single element of your production has the ability to affect the audience's psyche on such a deep level simply by *existing*. The power of the space is at your disposal.

3. Living Choices

In Chapter 1: Starting Out, I encouraged you to read the chapter that most interested you first. It's fair to assume that if this is your first stop in our Living... chapters, you've identified that some level of audience interaction is a big part of what draws you to making an immersive piece. Giving the audience a large amount of free will is a big step to take, and one that requires significant planning – you need to make sure that your world is robust enough to withstand whatever they throw at it, without revealing the man behind the curtain.

This chapter deals with a number of different Mechanics; systems that allow you to plan for the apparently unpredictable nature of an audience's free will.

Let's begin by defining how much power your audience is going to have – it's going to shape everything from your devising process to your rehearsal schedule.

My first suggestion is to break this sweeping idea of 'choice' down into separate performance elements. Simply saying 'the audience has free will' is a broad and largely unhelpful statement. *How* do they have free will? We already know there will be limits on what you want the audience to do in the production; presumably you'd rather they didn't show their independence by leaving halfway through and never returning.

Are your audience...

- Free to wander where they like?
- Able to converse with the cast?
- Meant to affect the story?
- All going to experience the same events, or will they have unique experiences?

These ideas aren't mutually exclusive, and you can answer yes and no to any combination of these. The crucial thing to remember is this: every element of free will you add to the piece will drastically increase the amount of planning you need to do.

Some of you will be excited by this. The idea of crafting a full, reactive world that sculpts itself around the audience really appeals to you, and you can see yourself surrounded by mounting stacks of annotated scripts, schedules and increasingly illegible napkins covered in scrawled pronouncements ('THE VICAR MUST APPROACH ALL AUDIENCE MEMBERS WEARING AN ITEM OF RED CLOTHING FOR THIS TO WORK!'). Good, all power to you – this chapter will make your job more streamlined.

For the rest of you, you've got something specific in mind. You've honed your focus, knowing already where the interaction is important and where you want the audience to have a more curated experience offered to them.

Taking a few minutes early in the production process to clarify how choice will be used in your piece will save you a lot of energy later on.

Crafting Interactions

Audience interaction is a difficult beast to tame. On the one hand, we have our goal of presenting an Elegant production; we want the audience to be immersed in the performance rather than constantly being reminded of its artificiality or breaching the limits of what we've planned. On the other, we have the inherent impossibility of trying to plan for an infinite number of potential audience interactions. It simply isn't possible to incorporate every permutation into the play whilst still retaining a prominent narrative thread. With every increase in the production's interactive capabilities, an increasing reliance is placed on the cast's improvisational abilities.

To find the 'sweet spot' between the extremes of a static, 'on rails' experience and a free-form melee with no structure, there's one question that I keep coming back to:

How do we make sure this is an interactive play, not an extended improvisation?

And, I suppose, what are the actual differences between them?

In an extended improv, there are limits to the structure I can create in advance. At most, I could create a sort of 'open world' experience, where I set certain conditions, plan an event or two to refocus the performance at predetermined points and give my cast general advice on how to improvise their roles. I would give my participants a scenario. They'd receive some background, maybe some advice on creating a character that fits in the world. I might plan those few defined events to shake things up (like killing off one of the characters played by the cast), but the story would develop largely according to the audience's actions. The outcome would be dependent upon them. If I needed to bring the audience into line – for example, when it was time for the experience to end – I'd unleash some form of *Deus ex Machina*[1] which will overpower whatever they were doing at that moment: the perimeter is breached by an enemy, or we discover that our leader is a spy, etc., etc. It might have themes that we'd be hoping to explore, but we could only create the environment for them and hope the audience heads down that route. This style of dramatic experiment is a theatrical experience, but not a curated narrative.

There is nothing wrong with the extended improv, but it's not immersive theatre (at least, not in the way I understand it). It lacks

---

1. 'The god in the machine', a term that means unleashing a narrative device so powerful that it renders everything before it meaningless.

the sense of plot, of structured narrative, that we associate with a written or devised play. So how do we bring these elements together? How do we marry the narrative structure of a play to the free-form interaction of the extended improvisation?

This brings us back to the idea that we will know exactly *how* we are allowing the audience to affect the play – and these abilities are called Freedoms. There will inevitably be a limit on the Freedoms you bestow on your audience, so we have a duty to make sure that the Freedoms they *are* given possess two qualities:

1. For the audience, the Freedoms should be meaningful. I mean this in every sense. The production should be impacted in some way by the audience's Freedoms.

2. For the cast and production team, the Freedoms should be manageable. There needs to be a robust and predefined methodology that allows us to process and incorporate the audience's contributions into the production *as they occur*. These are our Mechanics.

This chapter contains a variety of techniques that make interaction both meaningful and manageable. As well as explanations of these concepts, I'll be taking you through how I've used them in the past in *Caligula* and *Anima*. These pieces were interactive worlds, with *Caligula* based around an existing text and *Anima* being an original devised piece; so whatever you're trying to build, you'll hopefully see part of a similar journey in these pages!

Casting the Audience

This first section is focused on a particularly thorny problem associated with immersive stories that must end in a certain way.

If you're planning a production with profound audience interaction but require the plot to end in a predefined fashion, there's a big decision you have to make early on in the process: how are you going to get the audience to interact with the play without derailing the plot? If your play *must* end with the villain's defeat, or the lover's reconciling or... whatever it is you've decided on, changing that ending would ruin the telling of your story and the message of your piece. The story is set, and the audience can't derail it. It's a sticky dilemma you've made for yourself, one of the most difficult we can face in creating immersive work. Is it even possible to make a play like this truly interactive?

The answer, luckily, is *yes*. There's no 'one size fits all' model that will work here, but there is a resource already at your fingertips that will provide part of the answer: the play itself.

Let's break this problem down further and identify exactly what it is we're trying to do, sticking to the guideline we laid out in Chapter 1: Starting Out. Define each problem, and know exactly what you're trying to solve. As you'll remember from that chapter, one of our most fundamental aims is to present an Elegant production. Beginning from this principle, we can assume that we don't want the audience to be explicitly aware of when they're 'allowed' to interact. Ranged up against this, we've got the demands of your set storyline. So we're trying to:

- Give the audience a sense of free will...

- ...without artificial limits...

- ...in a way that can't break the play.

You will notice that trying to make those final two points coexist can cause a dilemma. To find a way across this tightrope, let's take a look at the world your play creates.

Choosing Factions

Any play takes place within a world, whether it's high fantasy or kitchen-sink drama. The story has context, an implied 'outside' where the characters come from before the play, and go back to when it finishes. All good directors are aware of this when they work on any production, but the immersive company needs to look in even more detail.

To find out how your audience can interact, ask yourself how people would interact in the world you're building. What social situations are unique to, and therefore evocative of, your world? Those situations are where we can place the audience.

Sounds obvious, doesn't it? And yet, when you get down to it, that's quite an involved question. How do we 'cast' the audience? It's always an option just to let them be themselves, and not ask them to take on any fictional role at all – some companies do exactly this, even giving them masks that remove their status as recognisable people. In the type of production we're discussing right now, one where we're looking for significant audience freedoms, that becomes difficult; can you sustain the narrative while several bemused theatregoers wander through the castle? Can a masked non-person take an active role in the experience without straining the credibility of the world? For specific pieces, the answer may be yes, but in this section we're presenting a Mechanic that should work for the majority of productions. Assigning the audience a 'storified' role makes their presence logical and enhances the immersion, even if they totally fail to live up to the expectations of those roles! We can call these roles Factions; this was the term I ended up using when this concept first reared its head while working on *Caligula*, and it's stuck ever since.

What you're looking for are social groups or frameworks that already exist in your created world. It's easier than it sounds, and every good story world suited to an immersive production has these scenarios in place already, no matter what plot it has... But to prove it, we're going to work through this together. Just to make things easy for you, I'm going to choose seven fictional works, and you're going to choose two (it helps if you know them well). Try to pick worlds that seem completely different from each other, then we'll go through them together. Leave your own production aside for now, as it'll help you to understand the principles of how this works fully before tying yourself to any specific plans.

- *Star Wars Episode IV: A New Hope* (film, George Lucas)

- *American History X* (film, Tony Kaye)

- *The Coast of Utopia* (play, Tom Stoppard)
- *Romeo and Juliet* (play, William Shakespeare)
- *Caligula* (play, Albert Camus)
- *Treasure Island* (novel, Robert Louis Stevenson)
- *A Song of Ice and Fire/Game of Thrones* (novel/TV series, George R.R. Martin)

Just to be clear, I'm not suggesting you could acquire the rights for every one of these properties. This is a cross-section of well-known worlds from different forms of media rather than a realistic list of productions you could create.

So we have our selection of worlds. Now we need to look at what already exists in those stories that we can use to do our job for us! We're looking for social groups that can become our Factions, and the best groups are ones that naturally stick to the following few rules already, before you have to do anything.

RULE 1: The Faction is already disciplined or controlled without the need for you to tell the audience their 'rules' in an out-of-character way.

This means you're looking for groups that already have their own code of conduct, shared beliefs or other controlling factor. These can be loose family connections, membership of an organisation, a common goal or a ruler they have to obey. Casting your audience in Factions like these means it becomes rewarding for them to play their part in a way that helps your piece.

RULE 2: The Faction is immediately evocative of your world.

Here, we're basically saying go for something interesting. What's the Flavour of your world? Why's it interesting? Very few people want to be the farmers when they could be the knights!

RULE 3: Individual actions within the Faction can't derail the central driving force of the plot.

It's the flip side to the second rule... You want an interesting role for the audience, but you don't make them the king! If you give them the power to derail the story from within their Faction, you're going to have a much harder job. One thing you'll really struggle with is if the audience's roles would realistically give them the power to order around the cast. That way lies madness.

With those rules in mind, try to come up with suitable Factions for the fictional works you've chosen. To clarify, this means that you are choosing a social group of characters that becomes your audience's 'casting'. If you're still unsure how to do this, carry on reading for some ideas.

Analysing Factions

These titles are wildly different from each other. Their genre, media format, plot, structure and era in which they were written and set vary greatly. Yet it's possible to find a thread that links how we'd approach them in an immersive project. In each of these stories, the driving plot takes place against the background of a huge number of supporting characters. Some are seen or represented in the work; the X-wing pilots in *Star Wars*, the warring families in *Romeo and Juliet*, the neo-fascist thugs in *American History X*... All supporting characters with their own imaginable stories, there because of the main plots (and necessary for it to occur), but not affecting it in any significant individual way.

Then there are the other characters whom we know *must* be there for the world to work, but whom we either only briefly hear of or simply never become aware of until we deliberately think about it. The ground soldiers that must exist in the Rebellion's army, the host of sympathetic young hotheads in *The Coast of Utopia* and the nameless sailors in *Treasure Island* all have equivalents in the world of your creation.

For everyone we've mentioned so far, we can assume drives, fears, abilities and personal plots that have depth and resonance (within their genre) but are incidental to the main narrative. That's our third social rule already ticked off! All of the examples we've given also hit the first and second rules too. Rather than coldly analysing them, let's lay them out. Here are some example Factions within which you could cast the audience in immersive versions of these works:

Star Wars	Soldiers in the Rebellion, awaiting their next mission; or the Imperial Senate, called to listen to the latest pronouncements.
American History X	Neo-Nazi followers of Derek and Cameron, summoned to a rally; members of minority communities awaiting acts of aggression by the thugs or vigilante groups intent on revenge.
The Coast of Utopia	Followers and admirers of the various revolutionaries in the play; or reactionary Russian aristocrats threatened by these new ideologies.
Romeo and Juliet	Members and allies of the feuding families; or members of the City Watch and the Prince's retinue.
Caligula	Junior senators of Rome; prisoners of Caligula or soldiers in the senators' bodyguards.
Treasure Island	Crew members on the ship.
Game of Thrones	Soldiers for one of the Houses; or courtiers in King's Landing.

All of these groups are directly involved in the action, but all are at the mercy of something greater within the story that dictates the consequences that might come from their decisions. The actions of *Caligula*'s senators and powerbrokers are beyond the control of these Factions, as are the desires and decisions of the leading Capulets or the heads of the noble families in *Game of Thrones*. Identify your supporting groups, and you've got a solid framework for audience interaction within a fixed narrative.

Audiences are unpredictable; while most of them won't go out of their way to break the boundaries, there's always the chance that one of them will. That's where Rule 2 kicks in. If you make their Factions interesting to play 'correctly', you give all audience members a solid reason to help your play succeed. Give them roles that would be listened to, and never make them so oppressed or downtrodden that they have absolutely no hope of being valued. Use your best judgement for this, and gauge where your audience's roles stand in comparison to the cast. If the cast characters are kings, don't make the audience peasants... But if the cast are merchants, peasants would be a fine choice. The key is in having the audience be on a social level that the main characters would be aware of, but have no real responsibility to.

Case Study: Caligula

Caligula was the first production where I used Factions, and it was also probably the most complex use I made of them.

Part of the basis for that production was the interplay of various power groups, and how they worked together and opposed each other to achieve their own goals. We were working at the very beginning of the Tory/Lib Dem coalition government, so this became an interesting concept to explore in the modern world, as well as in the playtext itself. The perception of the borders between political parties were more nebulous than at any time in my generation's memory and, whilst the political landscape has changed beyond recognition in the short time since then, infighting and political manoeuvres remain a fundamental part of our society today – indeed, the concepts in our staging of *Caligula* feel even more relevant now.

In *Caligula*, the scenario starts as a well-ordered administration experiencing a minor hiccup, and moves relentlessly towards a tyrannical regime in the absolute grip of crisis. The main catalyst for these changes is Caligula himself, an increasingly autocratic and brutal ruler, but most of the onstage action is presented by the senators who chafe under his reign. This situation provided us with the perfect background to explore what might happen to power groups as the crisis intensified. As major figures die, or shift allegiances, the groups (initially divided along ideological lines based on modern-day issues like tax, welfare and reproductive rights) would coalesce into larger entities based around more fundamental life-and-death problems.

Right from the outset we were aware that, handled badly, this could have been a cheap form of game that jarred with the quality of the original play. It took us a long time to develop the correct structure; not only were we choosing the right Factions for *Caligula*, we were actually developing the Faction concept for ourselves for the first time ever. We kept going even when it seemed impossible to solve the problem of casting the audience; we believed this concept could enhance the play. At the time, we were very keen to find something that could go hand in hand with our grandly written aim for the project: 'The audience should experience an active and emotional (yet critical) evaluation of our relationship to the text and the situation the characters exist within.'

We cast the audience as junior senators; low-ranking members of the government who had the right to be in the same space as the more important figures (written in the original text and played by the cast), but who had very little bearing on the important decisions of the state.

Within this single large Faction, we identified that smaller 'sub-Factions' could evolve. There was time for audience members to explore the viewpoints of the various major characters and align themselves with those they agreed with most. To make this feel immediate and relevant to the audience, we had set our play within modern-day London. Rather than talking about the old Roman provinces of Gallia, Britannia and Italia, the cast would discuss the future of Greenwich, Barking and Islington, along with current moral issues, such as the financial crisis.

The possibilities this concept gave us were truly exciting. By combining the idea of Factions with some of the Mechanics that are explained later in this chapter, we developed a structure that allowed the audience to experience truly meaningful relationships with the production. An audience member had the opportunity to ally themselves with a Faction espousing a particular financial agenda or moral opinion. Later, through the preconceived Mechanics we had written in to the production, a Faction could find itself subsumed within the larger 'Kill Caligula' Faction dominating the Senate by the end of the play. The audience member would find themselves fully implicated in a plot they had no intention of being part of. How would they react? Would they embrace their new role? Attempt to defect to another group? Try to slink into the shadows and hope to avoid taking action? Stay within this group but actively oppose its plans and argue for a third way?

These shifts in the nature of the Factions were relatively easy to achieve, as we had cast our audience in a role that firmly obeyed Rule 3 ('Individual actions can't derail the play'). The power and influence of the Factions were firmly centred on the cast members that led them. To destroy a Faction, we simply had to kill off the character that led it, or have them defect to another group. Even if the audience decided to cling on to the now-rudderless Faction, they would swiftly grow tired of being powerless and seek new allegiances. This ensured that, by the time the production reached its climax, we would end up with the exact Factions in play that we needed. The audience were free to choose their path, to have influence on the world and to feel significant; but some events were simply too large and fundamental for an individual to impact the result. This could lead to frustration, but it worked because the preset narrative provided them an outlet for that frustration; a large Faction coalesced that was entirely based around the aim of killing the tyrannical Emperor. The audience could choose their relationship to that Faction (supporting it or choosing to join the small group of dissenters), but crucially we had provided a structured Faction that already expressed those possible responses to Caligula's madness.

The larger actions of the cast, and how they related to the play, were predefined and immutable. Caligula would always die at the hands of the conspirators, and Lucius and Octavius would always end up leading this large group of assassins. What the Factions gave us was a series of small hothouses where audience interaction could be meaningful, impactful and subtly limited. Within these laboratories, the audience could engage with ideas and plans, and attempt to modify them. In some cases, there was the freedom to succeed in these attempts. However, for this to work, we had to be clever with the structure of the narrative. An audience would swiftly catch on if they realised that they were only able to influence small and inconsequential decisions. Throughout the play, we created new plotlines based on the backstabbing and infighting of the senators that felt incredibly important at the time. It wouldn't be enough for an audience member to have their say and be rewarded with just, 'Excellent, good, I will ensure Greenwich station is renovated like you suggest.' There needed to be immediate and tangible results beyond a metaphorical pat on the head. To make this happen, we used Paths, Junctions, Variable Cues and Sync Points (all of which are explained in detail later in this chapter) to create scenarios that gave real weight to the audience's actions. A sufficiently engaged and passionate audience member could start a chain of events that led to guards dispersing a rival Faction.

Because of these genuine results, it wasn't immediately obvious when the 'main plot' was kicking in. There wasn't a clear border between 'things you can affect' and 'things you can't affect', right up until the end stages of the production (by which point the events taking place were so huge that it felt *natural* that low-ranking senators had little power). When one of Camus' pre-written plot points occurred, the audience were free to try to influence the events unfolding. The incentive to be proactive remained constant because the audience always had the *feeling* that they could influence events, even when this was untrue.

This created another interesting emotional effect within the audience. Because they had grown used to possessing some power (albeit limited) within the factional struggles, their impotence within the larger events of the play created anxiety and displeasure. Crucially, it was clear that it was an 'in character' displeasure rather than the frustration of an audience having their freedom taken away. When Caligula's madness and tyranny became the dominant plot point, the audience felt the frustration of their agendas and plans being subverted rather than the frustration of becoming passive spectators to a show.

A real example from our run illustrates this perfectly:

Mereia, a mediocre senator, led a Faction. Certain audience members rose to prominence within this Faction by taking an active part in conversations and winning the favour of Mereia, thereby gaining cachet when interacting within its sphere of influence. Then Caligula had Mereia executed on a whim. The group, robbed of a senatorial connection to the halls of power, dispersed, and were grudgingly accepted within other Factions without even a vestige of the power they had enjoyed. Indeed, the more prominent they were, the deeper the distrust they were subjected to. Caligula's whimsical killing had caused them discomfort and ruined their standing. In general, these people engaged with the conspiracy to kill the Emperor in a much more enthusiastic and self-interested way than many of the other audience members. Though our play proceeded as it always had to, our audience felt as if things *could* have gone differently; this feeling spurred on their engagement.

Choosing Factions II

Before we move on to look at how these Factions can interact with your play, it's time to come clean – I lied when I said there were three rules. There is a fourth, and much more important rule.

RULE 4: Ignore these rules.

When you understand *how* and *why* these rules work, you can start rejecting them. It's important to understand why these groups work so well because you can then approach other kinds of Faction with open eyes. When you break these rules, you'll have a good understanding of what obstacles you're creating to overcome later. I might break Rule 3, and decide it'd be *very* interesting to make my audience kings and popes while the cast are mere dukes and bishops... But because I looked at these rules, I now know I'm going to have to plan for their ability to affect the story. Maybe I go the other way, and make them downtrodden peasants because it'd be exciting to see them rebel against the play and their place within it. Again, I'm armed with the knowledge of what problems this is going to throw at me.

Influence

Having the power to interact and shape a play can be intoxicating for an audience member; we're so used to sitting down and listening that a new, different dynamic is exciting. If you're going to manage what the audience throw at you, the production's non-interactive elements need to be just as engrossing! The first step in creating manageable interactions is making sure that the audience are never so bored that they become disruptively proactive when you haven't planned for it.

This means, and I'll say this repeatedly, that *the traditional elements of your show must be as honed and professional as the immersive parts!*

Let's assume you're going to make that happen and that you already know how to make your scenes compelling. Our next stop is looking at the interactive segments themselves. One of our first concepts here is Influence. This is simply a shorthand way of saying 'How extensively can this interaction affect the production?' It's how we distinguish the small-scale interactions that go on all the time from the large game-changing ones that profoundly affect the play. This isn't a binary choice (big or small) but a sliding scale. How you iden-tify and rate the Influence of your interactions is up to you, but one possibility is to consider how much work the cast have to do (both in rehearsal and in the production itself) to react successfully to that interaction. Strictly speaking, these are separate considerations, and in your early explorations of this kind of work you may wish to sepa-rate this concept into Impact (the level of work required by the cast) and Influence (the level of importance the interaction has on the production's progress).

Examples will be more helpful here... In *Loveplay*, audience members would often ask a cast member a simple question. That's a very small and easily handled interaction. It didn't have much Influence, as it couldn't really change the play very much (unless the cast member had decided to reveal the ending!). The Impact was also very low; we had rehearsed these types of conversations repeatedly. Interactions of this nature can occur at any point, especially in Interactive Worlds, and planning for them is covered in Chapter 4: Living Rehearsals.

Meanwhile, in *Anima*, there was a point where a group of audience members were able to choose between joining the evil corporation or the terrorists. Whichever they chose, it totally changed the play – but we had planned rigorously for both those eventualities. This apparently fundamental shift in the production's plot simply led into one of three different scenes, all of which were well-rehearsed. The next section of this chapter, Junctions, Paths and Threads, will go into detail about how you can plan for this type of story-changing interaction, but all you need to understand right now is that this choice had a limited number of outcomes: the majority siding with the terrorists, the majority siding with the corporation or a roughly even split between each group. Planning this interaction became relatively easy because there were fundamentally only three possible results. Accordingly, we would say that this interaction had a high Influence but only a moderate Impact.

In both of the previous examples, the Influence of those interactions was entirely desirable. We wanted to encourage those kinds of proactive and engaged behaviour – and when the result of an interaction is desirable, it will have a manageable level of Impact. The difficulty comes when the Influence is high but unwanted.

In *Caligula*, an audience member managed to bypass all our safeguards and tell the Emperor that the Senate were plotting against his life. This was *not* planned, and there was the real possibility of the production derailing. It had a lot of Influence, as Caligula would conceivably simply round up all the main characters and have them executed. This would obviously completely destroy the planned arc of our story. As a result, this interaction carried an extraordinary amount of Impact; the actors playing Caligula and his inner circle had to work as a group to keep the play on track whilst acknowledging the audience member's contribution.

In essence, the best interactions are ones with *higher Influence than Impact*. We want interactions that feel important and meaningful, but we want them not to tax the cast's mental energy too much when they occur. To help keep interactions manageable, there are some key points that will help you keep the Impact low.

Impact will dramatically increase when the audience have an open choice rather than a closed one. In the *Anima* example above, each audience member had a closed binary choice on who they would side with. When each audience member had made this choice, we ended up with one of the three possible outcomes explained earlier. The Impact is low, because every reasonable eventuality can be planned for. The audience, of course, don't have to be aware that the interaction is this premeditated (see the Choices section later on for ideas on how to make closed choices feel open).

You can also space out the more profoundly impactful interactions. It would be a mistake to allow one very high-Impact interaction immediately to follow another. Allowing the dust to settle after a profound shift in the production will let the cast analyse what is occurring in the space and adjust their thinking accordingly. It will also give the audience a chance to realise and live with the consequences of their choices. It can be tempting to bombard the audience with choice after choice, supposing that more options makes for more engagement, but allowing consequences to be felt is an important part of drama. An endless procession of options and choices with no breathing room can be an engaging experience, but it tends to erode the feeling of living within a story.

How you rate the Impact and Influence of interactions is up to you; what's important is keeping a handle on how much power your audience has at any time. If you've put a very impactful interaction in place, try to keep some time either side of it that is easily predictable. It's far easier to run a show with six equally spaced massive changes than to deal with three in a row. Your cast needs time to assess the new landscape of the piece and shift their performances accordingly.

Junctions, Paths and Threads

The most complex immersive pieces, Interactive Worlds in particular, have stories that reshape themselves according to the audience's actions. These productions take rigorous planning or the resulting confusion can be huge. These choices can have high levels of Impact, and we've already talked about how these need to be given space to breathe and settle.

Throughout my work in immersive theatre, I've been searching for ways to give the audience more and more power. The lesson I keep learning, over and over, is that increased freedom means the play needs to be more tightly structured. Every step that gives the audience a greater feeling of being in a free-form, living story, drastically increases the work of the company. This is very, very different to an improvisation.

Planning isn't just important from an organisational point of view; it's also necessary from an artistic point of view. Changes ripple through the play, building on one another to create results far from what was intended. If five minor interactions in the play are handled poorly, the audience will carry on with the play using whatever feedback they received as a guide. They will all arrive at the climactic events of your play with misconceptions, exercising choice and influence in ways you've failed to anticipate.

If your opportunities for real, influential choices aren't planned, then you cannot produce a dramatically satisfying climax. You may just about be able to improvise something that fits, but it will have none of the resonance or pathos that a planned resolution would.

In our work, we think in Junctions, Paths and Threads. Junctions are points where the play as a whole can be changed, whilst Paths are routes the audience takes to and from the Junctions. These routes may not be actual physical journeys through space – a Path is a narrative route through the story, a particular set of experiences, so someone can be on a Path whilst sat in a chair. Threads are ways of categorising how the production has changed in response to the audience taking certain Paths from certain Junctions. This sounds confusing, and it's easiest to explain with a real-life example.

Case Study: Anima

In *Anima*, the play always started in the same way. The audience went through an extended entry procedure, and met the shadowy Osiris Corporation. Half an hour went by where they had the freedom to interact, but the play carried along the same narrative (using terminology from earlier, the audience were in a Hub and their interactions had very little Influence). As this scene progressed, the audience were sent along different Paths – mostly through the techniques described later in the Choices section. Some ended up assisting the Head of Medical Research with his tests; some were identified as undesirable elements and taken to a prison holding area; others remained in the Hub and became part of the meeting where Osiris planned to take down the Network, a group of terrorists attacking them. These are all examples of Paths; different routes the audience took through the same narrative. Paths are mutually exclusive, as they happen simultaneously. The experimental group would not learn of the terrorists when the planning group did, for instance. You may have noticed that these Paths were also slowly Dividing the audience into Factions (prisoners, researchers, etc.).

Those audience members who had been taken to a prison area were being guarded, and these guards were subsequently killed by a terrorist. The terrorist then vanished… Leaving the audience alone, and with an unspoken choice. They could return to Osiris and tell them what had happened; they could follow the terrorist and be taken into her group; or they could remain where they were, being found by Osiris guards. There were small variations on these themes, of course – one audience member could rebelliously follow the terrorist against the group's wishes, which would trigger the terrorist's companions to capture the rest of the group. The end result, in terms of where the audience group ended up, was the same as if all of them had chosen to follow. Whatever they decided, this choice would send the whole play catapulting down different routes. If they returned to Osiris, the Corporation became aware that the terrorists were on the property and stepped up plans to counterattack. If they were discovered by Osiris guards, that information would reach the Corporation too late and enable the Network to attack them. If, however, they joined the Network then the terrorists would delay their attack while they tried to extract information from the newcomers.

This is an example of a Junction. The play's course was drastically affected by the Path the prison group chose at this Junction. The route the play *as a whole* takes after a Junction is called a Thread – so there is a Thread where the Network attack the Corporation, one where the Corporation learn that they're in danger, and a final Thread where the audience join the Network. The distinction between Paths and Threads is very important; the *Paths* that each audience member chose would dictate the *Thread* of the play that we were following in that particular performance. Once the production has been underway for a few scenes, the number of potential Threads can become quite large. Representing these visually is always helpful. Post-its and string on the rehearsal room wall are our usual weapons of choice!

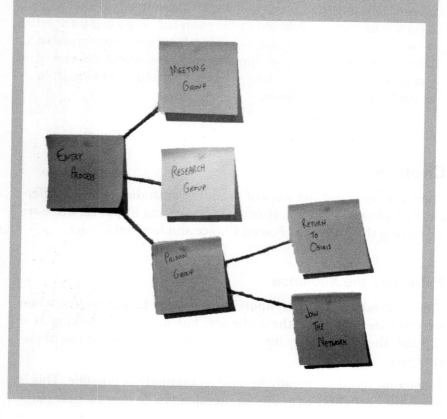

These Post-its show the first few Paths that audience members could have found themselves on. The final choice, stretching out from the 'prison group', would dictate which Thread the play would then follow as a whole.

Crucially, the audience would not have been aware of the difference between Junctions and Paths. They had no way of knowing that walking in one direction or the other would affect the play any more than their choice to join the Head of Medical Research or not. At all times, they are offered the ability to make choices. Every choice feels equally important at the time it's made.

When you're crafting your Threads, keep the outcomes manageable. In *Anima*, those three Threads we mentioned always still involved the test group going through their research. The planning group always remained in the main hall. They experienced different events, but the play didn't twist into an unrecognisable form. Remember, changes ripple through and affect the rest of the play. A series of moderately different Threads can amount to a drastically different climax.

Choices

There are three distinct ways of prodding an audience down different Paths from a Junction. In order of increasing Elegance, these are Extracting the Audience, Forced Choice and Implied Choice.

Extracting the Audience

This method was touched upon in Chapter 2: Living Spaces, when we discussed Dividing the audience, but here we're looking at it through the lens of story interaction rather than how we use physical space.

Extracting should generally be used as sparingly as possible. This is when the cast chooses audience members to go down a new path, without the audience actively choosing to do so. In *Anima*, the prison group were extracted by being arbitrarily chosen and escorted outside. This is best used early in the play, when people may not yet be confident leaving the rest of the group behind. It removes audience agency, so has dangers. Remember, you are teaching your audience how the play works at all times. It only take a couple of extractions to tell an audience member they don't need to take active part. Used effectively, however, it can throw your audience off-balance. One of my favourite tactics is to use this to separate groups of friends or family, especially if they're walking that fine line between having fun and attempting to derail the piece; we've found that removing the protection of their 'herd' can cause them to take a more constructive role. This should be done carefully, though. For some people the reverse is true, and a quiet audience member should probably be left with their friends.

Extracting can, used correctly, be very powerful. If you've built a piece where the Elegant choices are frequent and exciting, a little bit of extraction can provoke an emotional response that would be difficult to elicit in another way. Outrage at being detained, excitement at being handpicked by an important character and the elitism of being part of the in-crowd, can all be created by Extracting.

Forced Choices

Forced Choices are instances when the audience is overtly given options. It's less problematic than Extracting, but still a little clumsy. Our audience in *Anima* were given a Forced Choice when they were offered the chance to take part in the medical research. Again, though, it exposes the Mechanics at the heart of the play and encourages the audience to wait for permission to act.

When creating a Forced Choice, you need to remember that *refusing to choose* is a choice that should be planned for.

Implied Choices

The most Elegant option is the Implied Choice. In *Anima*, when our prison group were left outside, they faced an Implied Choice; they were not explicitly told to take action, but whatever they did would have a consequence. Obviously this is the most Elegant option because it doesn't point out the Mechanics of the play, but it's also the most artistically interesting. A Forced Choice will present options, and the audience picks from them. It's a multiple-choice question, with little scope for creativity. An Implied Choice is a free-form question, as you haven't explicitly laid out their options before them. Our prison group weren't told that they had three choices, or even that they had any at all, leaving it all up to their own judgement.

A fantastic result happened for us during this Implied Choice when our audience began to argue. A minority of the group wished to go with the Network, and their argument left them out in the prison area long enough for the Corporation guards to come looking... At which point some of the audience ran away to find the Network, followed by the shouts of the guards! The audience still with the Corporation in the main hall heard the shouting, and grew nervous. This kind of visceral reaction would never come from a Forced Choice, and only occurred because they were given what felt like true freedom.

The trick to managing this is subtly to limit the possible choices at the Junction without being obvious. We placed the prison scene in an area where there were only two directions to move in: forward to the Network or backwards to Osiris. The only other option was staying in place, meaning that all the audience could actually choose from were variations on three major Paths. This was easy to plan around, but felt much more liberating than overtly stating those three choices to them.

The limitations to the choices don't have to be Physical Boundaries like in this example, and the Implied Choice doesn't have to involve actual movement. Choosing whether or not to relay a certain piece of information truthfully to a character can be an Implied Choice – with the options being to tell the whole truth, tell a lie, tell a partial truth, or say nothing.

Using Choices

You may discover that your Forced Choices can be easily converted into Implied Choices. Originally, we had the terrorist overtly asking the audience whether they'd like to come with her. In rehearsal, it felt clunky. It also seemed that in performance, nearly every time, the audience would choose to go with the Network. The cast have a power over the audience, and if their characters express a preference in a Forced Choice then they will normally get their way. When we realised that removing specific instructions would still leave the audience with only three options, it changed the entirety of our piece. We started looking at the rest of the Junctions offered, and asking where we could remove elements of obvious instruction. Aside from making the play more interesting and free-form, it also started changing our audience. Those who chose to go with the Network became active and vocal participants. They had been taught, through the use of Rewards, to interact – in this case, the Reward to their proactive choice was the discovery of a whole other group of characters that no other audience member had yet discovered. I'll say it again... You are *always* teaching your audience how your world works.

The different types of choice can be combined, sometimes for very dynamic results. In the *Anima* example above, the Implied Choice can lead to an extraction if the audience stays and waits for the guards to find them. Any extraction actually carries an Implied Choice with it: 'What if I refuse?'

One final note about these choice Mechanics. None of them, right down to the most obvious extraction, should ever be out of character. Your play should be sufficiently coherent that all audience dynamics are delivered within the world you have created.

Variable Cues

Variable Cues will save your sanity. Plotting events across a free-roaming, interactive performance could be a nightmarish process if you didn't have a robust system in place to help the cast manage unexpected responses on the fly. Scenes will take different amounts of time each night, and audiences will vary wildly in their levels of energy and autonomous exploration. Yet your poor actors must perform their roles flawlessly, taking their cues from an audience that will never do the same thing twice. This is where the Variable Cue comes in.

Many immersive productions I've seen simply rely on one form of external cue, and the production's depth suffers for it. They will use time ('At 8:47, make sure the man with the gun enters the room from the side door'), audience dynamics ('When twenty people are in the small room, play the audio track'), or some other external factor to decide when the production moves on.

This always has gaps. What happens if, at 8:47, only a tiny segment of the audience are in the room for this climactic confrontation with the gunman? What happens if those twenty people reach the small room much earlier than anticipated and the audio track isn't long enough to keep them occupied until the next scene is ready? Issues like this are potentially show-breaking and are, I suspect, a large part of why many immersive productions dilute their level of real interaction.

The Variable Cue is a tool to fix this problem. Essentially, it's a set of logic commands like those a computer operates on. I can almost hear your incredulousness from here, but hear me out! Essentially, any action that's cued by the audience would be triggered by a combination of two or more cues. These cues can be anything, but common examples could be:

1. A previous section of script has been delivered.

2. A certain time has elapsed since the show started.

3. A certain number of people have entered a Zone.

4. A certain number of people have been drafted into Factions.

Everything can be linked with 'if', 'and', 'or' and 'then'. So *if* a certain thing has happened *and/or* another thing has happened, *then* another thing can happen. I first used these way back in *Caligula*, and have actually saved the receipt on which I scrawled my first Variable Cue. It reads...

IF!

section 6 of the script has happened

AND!

it is after 7:30 p.m.

AND!

the major Factions have all left the space

THEN!

Caligula can enter.

I genuinely cannot express how much of that play hinged upon these cues. They gave my cast a way of retaining control of the situation whilst still having room to manoeuvre. Although complicated on first glance, it's a simple system to enact. Actors are used to making sure previous dialogue has happened anyway, and it's no great difficulty to check the time. Ensuring a space is clear should be easy too. As long as no single cast member has too many cues like this in quick succession, you should have a production that is dynamic in its pace.

This allows the story to move along at a clip the audience can cope with, but also gives you the ability to hurry them along. You could, for example, use 'or' instead of 'and' in your equation. A Variable Cue for *Caligula* could read...

IF Scipio's Faction has broken up OR it is after 8:30 p.m. THEN the guards will go to Scipio's headquarters and disperse anyone found there.

This gives time for audience interaction to flourish, but also gives it a realistic limit that keeps the production moving. These changeable limits also create different experiences each night, as the process of mopping up the remnants of a Faction from a room is very different to breaking it up in full flow.

Sync Points

As the play moves forwards, and your audience explores different Paths, you will start running into time-management issues. Because they can ask questions and take action (or not...), your audience can affect the length of a scene. We've had a five-minute scene take fifteen minutes because the audience were engaging in a particularly active way. This has a knock-on effect. If one Path of the play is running ten minutes behind schedule, scenes that rely on it finishing on time are left high and dry, with actors having to improvise time-filling interactions on the spot without knowing quite how long they've got to wait. As with all interactive elements, the changes ripple through the piece; a ten-minute overrun early in the play can easily become a twenty-five-minute lag later on if it isn't brought back in union with the rest of the piece.

This is where Sync Points come in. A Sync Point is a scene that is designed to bring different Paths of the play back in line with each other. It is rehearsed in such a way that it could go on infinitely long, but can also be dispensed with in thirty seconds. Again, an example will be more helpful.

Case Study: Anima

In *Anima*, there was a scene where the Network took all their audience supporters to the Corporation's base to deliver an ultimatum. These supporters were coming from three different Paths, all representing different story reasons to become involved with this violent group. Each of these scenes was heavily interactive and, therefore, hugely variable in the times they could take. So we wrote in a scene where Skull, the leader of the Network, assembled her force before venturing to the base. As each group of audience members finished their previous scene, they arrived in the courtyard where Skull and her fellow leaders waited. There, they were prepared to interact for as long as it took for everyone to assemble. They spoke about the depredations of the Corporation, and made the audience feel truly special for having made the decision to leave them.

When the second group of audience arrived, our cast could relax slightly. Audience members who had last seen each other with the Corporation greeted one another in shock and pleasure. They started teasing each other, saying that they didn't think their friends would have had the guts to leave the safety of the base. The first time this happened, it was a wonderful moment for us. It proved that our world had taken hold of the audience, and that they were now fully invested in this story. When the third group arrived, we could sit back and allow the audience to do our work for us for a while. The cast listened, learning something of the relationships between audience members (fuel for a later scene, where friend would be turned against friend).

This is how a Sync Point works. It gathers Paths together in one scene, allowing the play to realign itself. In our example, this Sync Point led directly into another, larger one, when the Network marched into the Corporation to make its demands. This brought the entire audience together into the Hub for the first time since the Entry Process.

Entry Process

I've consistently hammered home that you always need to teach your audience how to interact. Nowhere is this more true than when they first enter the space, so the Entry Process is one of the most important scenes you'll craft.

How your audience enters the piece will provide them with a valuable piece of information: the Rules of Engagement. These are the instructions and permissions that they assume govern your play. As with many other aspects of immersive work, you cannot stop this happening. If you don't actively craft these rules, the audience will draw their own conclusions and create them for themselves. This leads to problems when they either don't interact in a sufficiently proactive way or misinterpret where and how they can take action.

By this point you presumably have a good idea of the level of interaction your piece is built around.

Your Entry Process will be built around two major pillars:

- Introducing the story.

- Introducing the Mechanics.

It needs to do these things clearly and, as ever, with Elegance. There aren't many hard-and-fast rules surrounding the Entry Process, being so reliant on the unique aspects of your piece. What I can give you are four examples of Entry Processes... Three that worked, but first: one that didn't.

Case Study: #MSND

In *#MSND*, our audience walked into the space without guidance. Ahead of them was a large nightclub space without actors. They filtered round the room, took up positions around the wall and waited passively for the performance to start. It started with a set scene of dialogue, followed by another. And another. Twenty minutes in, the music started. The majority of the cast entered. They danced, and wordlessly invited the audience to join them.

The audience didn't respond. Some jigged self-consciously in their spots by the wall, but no one came on to the club floor. We had left it too long; the audience had been taught that they could watch this performance whilst stood by a wall. In addition to the mistakes we spoke about earlier, our lack of Entry Process had removed control of the piece from our hands. The audience created their own Rules of Engagement, and they weren't the ones we expected. As you will know if you've read Chapter 2: Living Spaces, this also contributed to the creation of a huge, gaping Void.

Your Entry Process needs to be much, much better than this. It must pay attention to how you want the audience interacting, and introduce your world as something vibrant and alive.

Case Study: Anima

For *Anima*, our audience waited outside the 'Quarantine Centre' (our performance venue), unable to see through the blacked-out windows into the space. In small groups, they were let through into a small antechamber. Ahead, they could see the large hall that formed the Hub of the performance – but an armed guard sternly stood on the other side of the doors, blocking them from opening. The entry shut behind them, leaving them confined in a cramped space.

After a few seconds of confused waiting, small doors at the sides of the chamber burst open. Two guards in hazmat suits and gas masks entered and began examining the audience for signs of infection. They were asked medical questions, and their Osiris membership name badges were scanned and noted down. Meanwhile, the audience still waiting outside heard the screams of shock when the doors burst open but were unable to see what prompted them. A little cheap and cheesy, admittedly – but this was in our hometown, and we knew no immersive work had been performed there before.

When the audience were allowed to proceed from the antechamber, they were subjected to individual interviews with members of the Osiris Corporation. Their answers determined where they were instructed to sit in the Hub, and this decision was influenced by a combination of the answers given in the moment and information we'd gathered from them during the ticket-selling period several weeks before (more on this sort of process in Chapter 5: Living Beyond the Performance). In the Hub, they sat under the watchful eye of the security guards and waited for the rest of the audience to enter.

After the first two runs we sat down to assess the show, and the Entry Process was first on our list. It had achieved many of our aims – starting to turn the audience against each other, creating feelings of privilege and resentment. We had introduced the theme and rules of the world effectively, without any need for out-of-character explanation. The audience had also been left feeling intimidated by, and distrustful of, their hosts. It wasn't, however, an unmitigated success. The cast noted that they'd had to work very hard in the next few sections to provoke the audience to take independent action. Our Entry Process had battered them into submission, and created a Rule of Engagement we didn't intend: 'Do what you're told at all times.'

Through the run, we modified this section, introducing more opportunities for proactive choices from the audience. Small, low-Influence interactions such as giving the most privileged audience members tokens to spend at the 'canteen' (a bar staffed by an in-character cast member) and inserting more open questions into the interviews brought an element of proactive discussion back into the production from the outset. We eventually arrived at a good balance, and this Entry Process is one I still look back on with (malicious) glee.

Case Study: Loveplay

Being a free-roaming piece of Exploration Theatre, *Loveplay*'s Entry Process had entirely different requirements to *Anima*. Set within a time-hopping metaphysical dating agency, one that hooked Roman legionaries up with Georgian ladies, we endeavoured to create an experience that balanced two opposed but necessary qualities. We needed a Hub that was enjoyable to stay in, but also had to provoke the audience's desire to explore elsewhere.

The audience entered the space as soon as they arrived, pausing only to show their tickets at the reception desk staffed by a severe-looking nun. Within, they encountered a plush space bustling with life and characters, with decor inspired by the phrase 'Imagine if your gran ran a brothel.' A burly Viking sat in the corner, with a tattered Mills & Boon novel pinched between his beefy fingers. The bar was manned by a young World War I soldier and a Dickensian tavern girl. Characters bustled through and around the space, interacting with each other and the audience members. Staying and drinking in this bar/foyer was designed to be a theatrical experience in its own right, but the constant influx and exodus of characters to areas further in the space would lead the audience to question what was beyond the Hub.

This Entry Process, you'll have noticed, is far less complex and scripted than *Anima*'s. Knowing what your production needs is absolutely key; sometimes, apparent simplicity does the job far more effectively than complex procedures. But don't be fooled, there was still rigid planning behind the apparent chaos. Cast members were assigned specific tasks – encouraging exploration, helping confused audience members, world-building interactions... There is a very big difference between planned chaos and the real thing!

Case Study: Caligula

Caligula was the most challenging Entry Process I've worked on to date. It demanded the freedom of *Loveplay*, combined with the guided and curated experience of *Anima*. A tall order by any reckoning! As I mentioned in the section on Factions, we'd decided that the appropriate Faction for our audience was low-level members of the Imperial Senate. This gave us the starting point we needed to begin crafting an interesting Entry Process. As we were using the same space in which we previously performed *Loveplay*, we chose the Great Hall as our Hub.

The audience entered, and were immediately greeted by a room awash with important senators. They were met by servants who would greet them – these greetings would root the audience into the world of our play. They'd be asked questions about their area of origin and the issues facing it, being treated as an authority on their 'diocese'. Primarily, the audience were from within London, but others came from further afield; we used these distinctions to further differentiate the audience's experience. An audience member from outside London was treated as if they were from the wilder, uncivilised frontiers of the empire, a modern-day analogue of the Britannia and Germania of Roman times. They would eventually find themselves being canvassed by more and more important characters, including the main cast. They would gain an insight into the main loyalties and opinions of the central characters, and perhaps find themselves growing affiliated to one of these groups.

Behind the scenes of this apparently free-form politicking, a very rigid structure was in place. Our actors were divided into three distinct groups: the main cast and two groups of Floating Cast (a concept explained in Chapter 4: Living Rehearsals). Audience members would be dealt with by each group in turn, according to the following pattern:

- *Greeters/Floating Cast 1*: This group, generally in the role of servants and slaves, would greet new audience members and start to introduce them to their roles. By treating them in a respectful way and asking basic questions about their area of origin, the Greeter would lead the audience member towards understanding the world we had created and their part within it. Greeters had the capacity to deal with multiple audience members at once. They would attempt to break up groups of friends or family, forming groups of unrelated people. The Greeters would also attempt to draw out a political or societal issue that the audience member cared deeply about, ready to hand this information on to the next group of cast. As a side note, we originally settled on the idea that this group would be cast as slaves (which were, of course, common in Rome). In the end we discarded this; the risk of offence was great and it added nothing to the production. Controversy is something I'll happily risk, but only when it serves the aims of the production. This was not a production about the ethics of slavery.

- *Junior Senators/Floating Cast 2*: Serving as intermediaries, these cast members stood amongst the third cast group (described below) but subtly watched the first group. When it was clear an audience member had grown comfortable in their role (through engaging enthusiastically in conversations or walking freely around the Hub), a Junior Senator would approach them as if they had been awaiting their arrival. They would glean information about the audience's political sympathies from the Greeters, and use this information to ferry the audience member to the appropriate member of the *next* cast group. Actors would use their own initiative to place audience members in an appropriate group (thus beginning to form sub-Factions). For example, they may have placed a politically conservative but quiet type who was worried about immigration with a particularly reactionary Faction, reasoning that being placed within a mob that sympathised with them would draw them out of their shell. Conversely, they might have taken an outspoken left-wing firebrand to the same group just to start some fireworks. Although this section of the cast weren't the 'main' characters of the story, they had the most pivotal role within the Entry Process. They had to balance the experience of individual audience members with the overall dynamics of the production, making sure that the number of people in each starting Faction was roughly balanced. They also had to do this in an Elegant way; the audience's experience had to feel like being coopted by an ambitious politician rather than being shunted around by a production supervisor.

- *Senior Senators/Main Cast*: The main characters were the endpoint for the Entry Process. As the play progressed, these characters would be the focal points for the shifting alliances and power struggles that dominated the immersive elements of the narrative. Their role in this first section was to start forming roughly equally sized Factions by talking to (or ignoring!) audience members. Once the groups were fully formed, and the entire audience in play, a Variable Cue was used to trigger the entrance of Helicon (Caligula's right-hand man). His arrival would begin the first chunk of scripted dialogue.

The entry area was broken down into operational areas, through which the audience progressed.

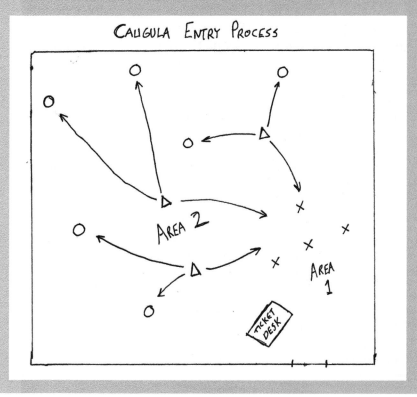

As seen above, audience would enter Area 1, a fairly static and reserved area dominated by the Greeters (X). Junior Senators (Δ) would ferry them to Area 2, an area of constant movement and bustle. Once they had decided on the right placement, they would move that audience member along to one of the Senior Senators (O).

After some time had passed, and as the Factions began to form, Junior Senators would do their best to distract audience members. By starting conversations with outlying members of each group, or insisting that 'You simply must meet Senator So-and-So' while walking them away, they would create movement between the groups. In this way, audience members had the opportunity to be exposed to each Senior Senator and their ideals. This opportunity wasn't mandatory, and audience members often decided they had found a Faction they were comfortable with before meeting every character.

This Entry Process was the most successful of the Case Studies. By allowing the audience total freedom, they invested in our world to a high degree. That freedom, however, was within a rigid structure that we had built. All our actors were fully aware of their specific function in guiding this process. This division of labour meant that freedom could be enjoyed whilst also providing guidance and in-character assurance to more uncertain audience members. The Rules of Engagement created by this framework continued to work in our favour throughout the production, leading the audience to invest and engage, but always within the constraints of the world we'd created.

An unexpected benefit of this process, one that I continue to explore to this day, was that it introduced a new idea: cast members could serve as Hubs. By introducing the audience into this whirling melee and having them attach themselves to a sympathetic cast member, that actor became the safest point in the space. As the play evolved and scenes started to disperse around the building, this meant that the audience's tendency to move back to the Great Hall (the most likely candidate for a Hub) was drastically reduced. This allowed us to use it as Caligula's throne room later on, a forbidding place that discouraged entry. Creating an incentive for some of the audience to follow their chosen actor-Hub into the nooks and crannies deep in the space meant that they grew accustomed to operating in those niches, away from the main halls of power. It enhanced the feeling of paranoia when, later, they found themselves part of a conspiracy to kill the Emperor.

What we can take away from all of these examples is that your Entry Process needs to keep a firm hold on what makes your piece unique. Setting your tone from the beginning is of vital importance. By the end of your opening, the audience should have learned about the world they're now in as well as the rules by which it operates. Craft your Entry Process diligently and your audience will help your production to continue along the same lines. Get it wrong and you may be shepherding them for the rest of the evening.

Tackling Prejudice

In all this talk about interaction and free-form drama, we need to touch briefly on the idea of prejudice.

Your piece may, as many plays do, address issues that are hot topics in society. You may be making a comment on racism, gender inequality, transgender rights, class-based oppression or any other topic that has potential relevance to the real lives of some audience members. Before you can wade into that dialogue, you have considerations that a traditional production doesn't.

Even if you're not tackling such thorny issues, the opportunity for a cast member to make an offhand comment that causes offence exists in any piece that allows for unscripted dialogue. In a scripted, traditional play, every word has been crafted in advance. Each syllable of dialogue has been weighed, judged, edited and rewritten until the exact message that the playwright desires has been expressed clearly and (hopefully) sensitively. You are about to launch a project where the cast sometimes makes up dialogue on the spot. They may have to riff on the themes of race, gender and class – or they may be talking about something completely frivolous and let slip a phrase they never realised was offensive to some groups. I'm sure you can see where the potential issues lie. In every single interaction, the cast become ambassadors for the ethics of your company. You must ensure that these issues have been addressed in the rehearsal room. Ensure that the whole company is on the same page as each other in terms of these opinions on these matters, and that you've agreed on language. Words have power, and can either liberate or oppress. Make sure your language is consciously chosen, and that the effects you have are those that you plan rather than those you accidentally stumble across.

Avoiding controversy isn't the goal here; communicating your intent clearly and sensitively is. Even if you make sure you adhere to this, you may encounter criticism. When you do, consider each piece of critique fully and individually. Once done, you can choose to disagree, clarify your position, stand by your point whilst acknowledging it was communicated badly, or outright revise your position and apologise accordingly. Avoid false apologies. 'We're sorry you were offended' means nothing. Be aware of your origins, and your privilege; don't be the man who lectures women about feminism, or the white person who tells people of colour that racism is no longer an issue.

Game Theatre

Game Theatre, for want of a better term, could fill a book all of its own. It's a distinct genre, though shares many characteristics with immersive performance. As with so much of what we've discussed, it's difficult to draw a defining line between where one form ends and another begins, but to me the principal difference is its approach to rules. In immersive theatre, I've hammered home this idea of Elegance – the idea that the 'rules' should be hidden and intuitive, preventing them from getting in the way of the performance. In Game Theatre, the rules often *are* the performance. They may be obvious and told to the audience before they start; they may be hidden, with the audience having to discover them. Either way, many of the rules are designed to be known, and that knowledge enhances the enjoyment of the piece. The Mechanics are designed to be directly enjoyed by the audience, rather than subtly underpinning the audience's experience.

I've elected to discuss it within this chapter, as interaction is the crucial mechanism that makes it work. If you're interested in learning more than this snippet, I can heartily recommend investigating the work of Hobo Theatre (www.hobotheatre.co.uk) – Artistic Director Jamie Harper has been exploring this kind of performance in much greater depth than I aspire to.

Designing Game Theatre

If you're going to make Game Theatre, you're trading Elegance for an obvious ruleset with which the audience engages. As we've spoken so often about the difficulties of keeping things Elegant, you may think this will be an easier job... Sadly, it's not! The chief reason we keep the Mechanics hidden in immersive productions is that the Mechanics simply aren't as interesting as the worlds we build. Making Game Theatre isn't just a matter of putting those same Mechanics out in the open – if it was, we'd simply be making a clumsy, uninteresting form of immersive theatre.

In Game Theatre, the Mechanics themselves need to be fascinating to explore. They need to offer Freedoms within a rigid set of constraints. They need to be as rich and diverse as the worlds we build in immersive theatre. They need to offer Flavour and context, not merely a framework for action. It's a tall order.

Right back in Chapter 1: Starting Out, you wrote a Mission Statement that would guide your piece. A similar idea will help here. Decide what you want your audience to do or experience. You have total freedom here, but try to keep it focused. Some ideas, cribbed from Game Theatre I've seen or worked on, are...

- I want the audience to deceive and backstab each other.
- I want the audience to build alliances to reach a common goal.
- I want the audience to work hard to discover the rules.
- I want the audience to realise they can break the rules.

All of these starting points, and the infinite number of others you can concoct, give us a point on the horizon to focus on; if we adhere to the central experience we're aiming for, we can ensure that all rules are built to enhance that ideal.

Rules Bloat

When we begin talking about Game Theatre, we need to acknowledge that there have been practitioners of this kind of interactive entertainment long before the mainstream theatre community started acknowledging it! Delving into the worlds of LARPs (Live Action Role-Players), Urban Games and even board and card games can open us to a wealth of experience that doesn't necessarily exist within our field.

One of the concepts bandied around in board game and LARP system reviews is 'Rules Bloat'. This means burdening the player with excessive rules that seem to hamper, rather than enhance, enjoyment of the experience. We live in the perfect time to watch a process of natural selection happening that proves this concept; and you need look no further than Kickstarter and other crowdfunding sources. Many, many games have found success or failure through this medium, and often they will offer some kind of preview version to allow people to try out the rules. A quick trawl through the forums at a dedicated website, such as Board Game Geek (boardgamegeek.com), will provide you with the dominant opinion: there is a fine line between a game that is too simple and too complex.

Rather than going into a long tract on the philosophy of rules in board games, here's my selection of lessons we can draw into our theatre productions. If you're interested in more in-depth discussion, I encourage you to explore the websites I've referred to and to run some web searches for 'Urban Games', 'Nordic LARP' and 'game design'.

- Rules should be easy to understand – otherwise your game will break down.

- Rules should be designed to work quickly – if applying the rule to an action takes longer than the action itself, it's dull.

- Not everything needs to have a rule – only write rules for things that *must* be regulated.

- There can be hidden Mechanics in addition to the visible ones if this helps the piece to run more smoothly.

Most of the great Game Theatre I've seen or been involved in has been through a period of playtesting. Invite your friends to try out each iteration of the game, and invite their feedback. It is *very* unlikely that you'll hit on the perfect ruleset in your first try.

Leaving Choices

With all these possibilities, the one constant is meticulous planning. Keep notes, draw charts and back up your hard drive. I've ended up, repeatedly, with bedroom walls covered in sheets of paper connected by string – and it's incredibly satisfying to look at what you've planned and know that there will be people in the audience who won't have experienced anything like it.

4. Living Rehearsals

This chapter will probably be of most interest to the directors and producers among you, as we'll be dealing with the practicalities of scheduling, managing the actors' workload and successfully casting an immersive production. There are still, however, relevant points and ideas for actors, students and all other readers – if this is you, I hope you'll find it readable and interesting anyway!

Dividing Your Time

Rehearsing a piece of immersive theatre can, depending on your structure, be a very time-intensive process.

Does your piece allow the audience freedom of movement? Are there multiple scenes occurring at the same time throughout the space? Can the audience interact with the characters? Answering 'yes' to any of these questions will increase the amount of rehearsal you need. Answering yes to *all* of them can take you to the edge of despair (trust me, I've been there) before this process is through... but that doesn't mean you shouldn't do it!

For this chapter, I'm looking squarely at the most complex pieces. The more realistic among you can take the parts that are relevant to your piece then chuckle pityingly at the poor souls having to do all of it.

Preparing the Script

Before auditions begin, and your cast is confirmed, you need to prepare for the rehearsal period. If your play involves a script, one of your jobs is to prepare this for an immersive performance.

By now you should have looked at your space in some detail, and hopefully you've begun to get excited by the possibilities it offers you, and to examine its Flow if it's a multi-room space. Your job now is to decide where each scene is happening. Whether it's in the entrance room, deep in the bowels of your space, or on a walk between two corners of a large hall, making these decisions early matters a great deal. It forms the skeleton of your structure, the spine from which all the organic free movement will grow.

It may be that scenes from the play get divided up or joined together as you're preparing for an immersive piece. Sometimes, there is room for a 'break' section in the middle of a scene – where the scripted action stops and the audience interacts freely with the cast and each other. Don't worry about limiting yourself; it's pretty easy to change one of these settings later in the process. Changing your mind about one scene is a lot easier than going in without any decisions made in the first place.

Make a visual tool for yourself to help with this process. I tend to create spreadsheets, but you could just as easily work with spider diagrams, flow charts or Post-it notes on a wall. However you do it, note down where each scene happens, and the order in which they occur. If you have scenes taking place simultaneously, make sure you've noted that down too. You're looking to record three primary things:

WHAT happens WHERE and WHEN?

For our immersive production of *Loveplay*, my spreadsheet ended up turning into a monster. On the vertical axis, I plotted times. On the horizontal, cast members and their brief character descriptions. In the boxes where they met, I wrote in what action was occurring and where they were. Though it became enormous, this spreadsheet allowed me to check *what* was happening *where* at any given *time* with a very brief glance. Because I knew my space, I was able to visualise what areas were free and clear in which to craft some interesting side-scenes.

With this done, you can start to see where you're allocating your most precious resources: the actors. Against each scene, note down which actors are needed and which are available. You'll start to see when you have a large number of unassigned actors who can help your piece feel populated and interactive. In *Loveplay*, I became aware that the Saxons were free for a lot of the running time. Keeping this in mind meant that I could begin crafting side interactions with them that actually ended up adding a whole subplot to the play. Laying all these considerations out visually means that you'll catch these little details. It's so easy to overlook a vast resource when all your information is just in the forms of words or, worse, thoughts.

By the end of this process, you'll have an invaluable resource for your audition, devising and rehearsal periods. It is absolutely worth the initial effort, and you will lose count of the number of times you'll be grateful to have this at your fingertips.

Casting Decisions

Something to consider early on is how large your cast needs to be. For those of you rolling your eyes, this isn't as obvious as it may first appear; your cast may be much, much larger than the named parts your play calls for. If your named parts need to be constantly ready for their next scene, who are the audience interacting with? Who's demonstrating the ways they can interact? Who is inhabiting an obscure space that the adventurous audience members might discover? You may also, especially in your initial forays into immersive theatre, have *fewer* actors than you'd like. In this scenario, judicious use of your actors (facilitated by the spreadsheet) and attention to the use of the space will help you stretch your resources.

Floating Cast

The Floating Cast are actors who only take part in the interactive and improvised sections of the play. You might wish to audition them differently to the main cast (more on which later), as you're looking for a different set of abilities. You're looking for artists who revel in the chaotic nature of this role, but who can also keep a close eye on the progress of the play as a whole. One of their primary functions will be to guide events back on track if something happens to derail the piece.

When you're deciding how many of these you need, keep the style of your piece in mind. Exploration Theatre tends not to need as many as a full Interactive World, because the opportunities for audience Influence are fewer.

You might decide that the Floating Cast don't need to join the rehearsals until later in the process, giving you time to rehearse the main events of the play without worrying about underutilising some of your actors.

Casting

Obviously, you're going to have to cast your production. All of the usual rules apply, and I'm not going to go into the basics of casting any kind of play here. Instead, we'll look at what extra considerations an immersive casting needs.

First up, the audition itself – it is almost completely useless to cast this kind of production with a monologue audition. You need to find actors who can react at a moment's notice and are comfortable with the interactivity of the production, and all you'll find out with a traditional fifteen-minute monologue-based audition is whether they can perform something they prepared earlier. How you find your cast is up to you, but I've had the best experiences by running workshop auditions. Divide your audition into sixty- to ninety-minute slots and invite ten to fifteen actors to each session – not only can you see more actors in that time frame, you can put them through a process that allows you to gauge their comfort with interacting and improvising. Just as importantly, it can build goodwill; even those who don't get cast will hopefully have had an interesting day. Actors spend time, effort and money getting to and from your audition. It makes sense to ensure the audition itself is a worthwhile event to attend. If you're lucky, they'll tell their other actor friends how enjoyable your audition was. Admittedly, there are some actors who intensely dislike workshop auditions; this is a shame but you can't please everyone, and it could be a warning sign that they're not particularly comfortable with interactive work.

By the time you start running your auditions, you'll need to have your character breakdowns ready. These should include all the information that a more conventional theatre production would, along with some specific points for an immersive piece. If you're constructing a piece where the audience and cast can interact, one of the most important parts to get across is *how the character interacts*. What's their default attitude towards the audience? Understanding this will enable you to cast correctly in your workshops.

Case Study: Caligula

Here's an example character breakdown I used for my immersive reworking of Albert Camus' *Caligula*:

> Caesonia is young, intelligent and devoted to Emperor Caligula. Unlike Helicon, however, she has no great love for his cause. She fervently hopes, right up to the moment of her death, that Caligula can find happiness and peace; ideally, she would be part of that life.
>
> She is a courtesan to the Emperor, a position simultaneously of very privileged and very low status. She is mannered, intelligent and sensual, and wants to believe the best of humanity. Her moral fortitude is, perhaps, less solid than many of the other characters with whom we sympathise.

> She doesn't believe in this cause like Caligula or Helicon, but she doesn't stand against it like Scipio or Cherea. Her excuse may be love, but Scipio struggles with a similar affection.
>
> Despite this, Caesonia is capable of steeling herself to brutality. Her attitudes towards the senators by the third act are harsh and largely unyielding (though she does soften some of the terrors – for example, by revealing that the penalties for losing in Caligula's poetry contest are not too extreme). It seems that, though she doesn't believe in his philosophy, she has resolved to be the strength that Caligula needs. She abandons her will to his in public and reserves questions for their private moments.

That's as detailed as you would ever need to go; *Caligula* was very interactive and had a philosophical basis. In that breakdown is all the information an actor would need to start improvising interactions as Caesonia; but, crucially, there's still room for them to bring their own insights to the character. It's a fine line to walk, and what you should be trying to do is give the actor an idea and seeing how far they can run with it.

You could go into great detail about the kind of qualities that the actor requires for this role, above and beyond the usual skill set desired for a traditional play, including the kind of interactions you've planned. I think this puts off potentially superb actors who have no formal experience in improvisation or interactive work. Cast the net wide and you may meet an actor who is perfect in ways you never considered.

Auditions

Give some thought to how you run your auditions. Something I find useful is to decide on some of the themes of my production, then create improvisational workshops that show me something of the auditionees' ability to run with an idea whilst remaining safe and in control.

In *Loveplay*, we were dealing with simultaneous themes of love, repression and sexual violence. It was important to know I had a cast who could handle these issues sensitively when improvising in scenes that involved these themes. My workshop with them touched on these areas and didn't actually go anywhere near the source material. My auditions for *Caligula* looked at the political and philosophical themes, and stayed equally far from the script. One exercise we used were creating debates where the auditionees were expected to convey ideas they didn't necessarily agree with.

Interrogate, with real vigour, what you actually need from these auditions. Does gauging the actors' ability to deliver a prepared monologue from the text trump all the other considerations of an immersive piece? Refer back to your Mission Statement from the first chapter.

The Rehearsal Process

A good immersive piece pays as much attention to the quality of the acting as any more traditional play would. Balanced with that, however, you have additional elements to your play that you have to squeeze into the same rehearsal period.

I have three main tactics that help achieve everything within the limited rehearsal time you might have. These are:

- Variable Cues.

- An Autonomous Company.

- The Two-Strand Rehearsal.

Variable Cues cropped up earlier on in Chapter 3: Living Choices. For now, we'll start with the Autonomous Company.

An Autonomous Company

An Autonomous Company is one where everyone involved in the piece is capable of working to improve the play without permanent oversight from a director. There simply isn't enough time for one person to be intimately involved in every second of every bit of rehearsed work. Therefore, we should aim to build an Autonomous Company and let them loose.

Every cast is different, but there are several unifying traits all actors in this style of troupe share. The Autonomous Company:

- Understands and agrees on the end goal of the piece.
- Works efficiently.
- Gets ideas on their feet as soon as possible, rather than getting bogged down in table discussion.
- Ruthlessly dissects their work *after* it's been on its feet.
- Isn't precious about its ideas, and can accept a cut and move on.

If you can hone your cast into an Autonomous Company, it will do more than save you time; it will improve your play beyond what you would ever be capable of alone. Even if you were able to be in three places at once, you are simply one artist with one viewpoint. The best directors understand that the cast will bring new insights and new directions. In a performance so rich with possibilities, this can only be heightened in immersive work.

Throughout the Two-Strand Rehearsal process, aim to achieve an Autonomous Company; choose a cast that you feel comfortable sending off into another room with a brief. Consider each and every last one of them your assistant director, and watch as their increased ownership of the piece pays dividends.

Two-Strand Rehearsal

The Two-Strand Rehearsal is a method designed to keep the different demands of your process distinct, allowing you to keep track of exactly what has been done. When there's so much to think about, it's easy to get sucked in to spending three weeks on one set of interactions then realising you don't have a play at the end of it. So this method breaks the production into two elements: Concrete and Interactive Strands.

The Concrete rehearsals deal with the static elements of the production; rehearsals based on scripted, choreographed or otherwise set pieces of performance that need to remain largely the same throughout the run. Lines that must be delivered, movement pieces that must occur, and other performance elements of that nature, belong in the Concrete Strand.

The Interactive Strand is based around things that are more intangible, such as how the cast interacts with the audience and the possibilities they have in the space. These things need a very different kind of process, and in the early phases of rehearsal it's helpful to keep them separate. That way, you can merge them later on when both have some kind of structure and form.

It's worth mentioning that many companies have engaged in a more fluid process. It's quite possible to do this, but you do need to keep in mind how complex your piece is going to be. Many pieces we would call immersive don't go anywhere near the most involved ideas we're discussing here. How you run your rehearsal is always up to you and your company, but I would suggest starting with a clearly defined process that can become more free-form if you decide it's appropriate – it's much harder to impose a new structure on a fluid process.

Scheduling

Early on in our careers, including when we're students, we often don't have the luxury of all-day rehearsals throughout the week. Rather than giving you a weekly timetable that may not suit your schedule, I've broken down the process into seven phases. You can assign these phases however much time you think your production needs, but they're a good way of making sure you're hitting certain benchmarks before you move on to more convoluted territory. I'll provide some guidelines in the description of each phase, but you know your specific piece far better than I do.

When you're scheduling rehearsals, it's important to keep the two Strands (Concrete and Interactive) separate at first. You can assign separate rehearsals, or alternatively define times when you leave one Strand and begin another within the same session. It'll make your targets and progress easier to monitor.

Keep track of who is rehearsing a scripted scene in each proposed rehearsal session. All cast not being used for a scripted session should be given a brief for Interactive Strand work, ensuring that everyone's time – especially your own – is utilised efficiently.

Phase 1: Before Rehearsals

As soon as you've offered your cast their roles, get a copy of the prepared script (if you're using one) and character breakdown to them. Do this as soon as possible, so they have plenty of time to ingest the role (or roles) they're taking on. In addition to all their normal preparation, such as reading and learning the script, they'll need to understand the breakdown well enough that they come in ready to improvise for the immersive sections.

Help them out with some research pointers. Tell them about everything that has inspired the piece thus far. When we were rehearsing *Anima*, we pointed our cast towards...

- Books like *1984* and *Brave New World*.
- Films like *Blade Runner*, *Logan's Run* and *Metropolis*.
- Video games like *Fallout 3*.
- Music by *Aphex Twin*.

These common reference points meant that the cast understood the atmosphere of the piece in a real and visceral way when they arrived at the rehearsal room. It informed the choices they made from the very beginning, meaning that our time was used more efficiently than might otherwise have been the case. Whilst it would be unrealistic to expect every member of the cast to explore all the stimuli we offered (some people really don't like video games!), a grounding in this material establishes a common vocabulary of tone, themes and style.

You should aim to arrive at rehearsals with at least a vague understanding of *how* your production will be immersive (which Freedoms the audience will be given). Some thought should have been given to the concepts in the previous two chapters, Living Spaces and Living Choices.

Phase 2: Early Exploration

Your company meets for the first rehearsal! Congratulations; even getting this far means you've done a hell of a lot of work already. You're ready to begin your Two-Strand Rehearsals. For this early phase you do need to go through the Strands in a certain order (Concrete then Interactive) so that everyone is on the same page.

Concrete Strand

If you're tackling a production with a pre-written script (whether written specifically for this piece or an immersive adaptation of an existing play), read through the script together. By now, you'll have your prepared script ready along with the location of each scene. If it's a pre-existing play, you'll also be able to help the cast understand how the script's structure may have changed for this immersive rendering of the piece.

Encourage your cast to do this readthrough on their feet. Early on, you want to cement the idea that mobility is important in an immersive piece. There's no divide between audience and stage, so the actors' freedom of movement is much greater than it ordinarily would be. It also means that micromanaging their movements, or 'blocking' them, would be incredibly difficult. Let them enjoy this freedom early on; later on in the process, you'll end up helping to modify their movements slightly rather than trying to cajole an inert cast to move!

If this production is entirely devised, this particular phase doesn't significantly differ from any devising process. However, you should bear in mind that in later phases it will become very difficult to incorporate major changes to the play successfully. It will be very helpful to nail down *what* is happening in the play relatively early in the process.

Interactive Strand

After your readthrough, sit down with the cast again and talk through the story. Have an open discussion about what an immersive structure could add to this play – make sure they're on board with your concept. If it's a pre-existing play, discuss where the immersive elements will add to the play, what problems this might throw up, and elicit suggestions from them. Encourage them to take part-ownership of the project (thus beginning the process of forming the Autonomous Company) – it's too much for one artist to manage everything alone.

With all of this done, you can move on to the first bit of real creative work. If you're using a pre-scripted text, you may have already mapped out your scenes in the manner explained earlier, but it could be that you're working in a more collaborative way. If so, here's a structure that could help...

Break the play into broad segments, chunks of action that happen in the same time and place. These might be predefined scenes, but your pattern may be different. If this is to be a devised piece, try to decide on some important story events that you'd like to include at this stage; it is impossible to work on your Interactive Strand without any frame of reference. However you slice it, you will end up with a set of Nodes: quick events that have to happen for the plot of the performance to advance.

If we were putting on an immersive rendition of *Hamlet*, we might identify his encounter with his father's ghost as a Node. We might plot in the killing of Polonius, the suicide of Ophelia and the climactic deaths at the end of the play. These are all pivotal points that shift the narrative.

Lay out your Nodes in a visual way that the cast can look at freely, perhaps on the wall as a timeline. Then it's time to get your cast back on their feet. Forgetting the script, the cast now improvises the story of the play. The only things set in stone are the Nodes, and everything in between them can be played with freely. Allow them to take their time with the unstructured parts, but feel free to prod them towards the next Node if the action starts to lag. All actors are constantly engaged in the process, and allow them to use different parts of the room as multiple settings (while Hamlet contemplates the way forward on his own, the rest of the world carries on). Once this runthrough is finished, gather round and discuss what was discovered. Then run it again, this time specifying that they must not repeat any of the improvised sections from last time. Again, analyse this when finished.

This method of working is based on Active Analysis, a development of Stanislavsky's later work – if it interests you, there's many books on the subject. But for now, going through this improvised/structured exercise will help you immensely moving forwards. The individual actors will have found more of the inner life of their characters beyond what has been scripted for them, an essential tool when they're interacting with the audience. You'll also have started to cement the techniques of using free-form role-play that has a specified destination. This is the very nature of interactive performance.

If you're looking to explore a Guided Experience or Interactive World piece, you can eventually perform a version of this exercise where you and anyone else in your production team take on the role of the audience. You can purposefully derail the characters or probe for greater detail, giving the cast valuable practice for the real thing. Obviously, this is all done with the aim of helping the process and empowering the company; at this stage, if you do derail it, make sure it's in such a way that the actor has a viable chance of salvaging the situation.

Phase 3: Establishing Structure

This phase moves the process from free-form exploration to the skeleton of a production. By the end of Phase 3, your Concrete Strand sections should ideally be set in stone. The devising work, if your production involves any, should be done with the actors starting to feel confident in the shape of the scripted scenes.

Concrete Strand

In this phase, the usual work of a director takes place. Rehearse your scenes with the usual care and attention to detail, and never let the freedom and excitement of an immersive piece distract you from the rigour that a play always requires.

You will need to know where in the space the scripted scenes are happening by this point. You'll have to factor in a mobile audience and the dimensions of each space, so keep an eye on these considerations. Try to maintain the separation between the Strands during this phase; paying attention to the space and lack of fourth wall is not the same as factoring in interactions! Make sure that the cast and production team all visit the space together at some point in this phase of work (assuming you're not rehearsing there anyway). If you are rehearsing in a different location, it can be helpful to rearrange the rehearsal room regularly. It's easy to fall into the trap of seeing a particular direction as downstage, for example.

Interactive Strand

This is where the nitty-gritty of your immersive work starts. Right off the bat, hot-seat your actors. Make sure they know their characters inside out, and can voice their opinions on topics both important and mundane. What's their morning routine? What's their stance on poverty in their society? Everything that gives backbone and life to these characters will pay dividends in the work to come. If your piece has a heavier physical basis, you can 'hot-seat' the movement aspects of the work too. The sheer variety of physical work means I can't give you a set process to undergo, but it will be important to test how your actors' physical work can respond to new stimuli whilst keeping coherent with what you have devised together.

Start looking at the Entry Process. What is the audience walking in to, what are the characters doing, and how do your Factions (if you're using them) get created and start to make themselves felt? Improvise this, and any other large non-Concrete sections. Alternate between observing with an outside eye and being an audience member. Depending on the size of your cast, you may have to get creative with how you give the actors a taste of what the audience will bring to the space. Have them take on audience roles, and bring in any outside artists you know who may find this an interesting process – they may enjoy being your guinea pigs and wreak gleeful havoc on your Entry Process.

If your piece can develop down multiple Paths, and especially if it may have multiple possible endings, this is the week where you start to hone in on the Junctions in your production. Look at the Mechanics of how the audience can send the piece down one route or another. Whether this piece has Junctions or not, start moving towards a more fixed structure, using the idea of Nodes to form a roadmap for your actors. Each of these Interactive Strand sections form their own Nodes, and can be placed between and alongside your Concrete Nodes.

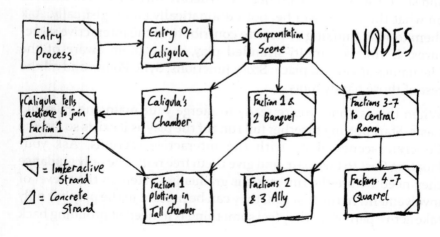

Phase 4: Honing Structure

Concrete Strand

The Concrete Strand should now be ready for polishing and honing. Start running the scenes back to back and satisfy yourselves that the heart of the play is ready for an audience by the end of Phase 4, working on individual scenes as required.

Inviting people to watch a run of this would be a very good move, showing your work as if it weren't an immersive production – one possible way of doing this is to show runthroughs of each of the possible Threads (from Chapter 3: Living Choices). Listen to their feedback. It can be tempting to brush off concerns with 'Oh, when the immersive things are in place it will all make sense.' This is a fallacy; if the Concrete heart of your play isn't artistically engaging or sufficiently professional, you will merely be layering an immersive framework onto a substandard piece.

Interactive Strand

If you're using a Floating Cast, now's the time to bring them in. While your main cast rehearse and run their scenes, you can begin drilling these new arrivals. Let them watch one of the Concrete runs, and start discussing the immersive structure with them. Fill them in on what their roles will be, both dramatically and logistically. Ask them to start thinking of ways to contribute to the interactive structures. If this is a multi-stranded play, make them aware of the Mechanics already in place: Story Junctions, Sync Points and all the rest of those handy tools.

When this is done, you're ready to merge your main and Floating Casts. Start putting together full runs of the play as it exists so far; the Concrete scenes along with the Interactive sections. Ask your Floating Cast to take part, and give them free rein. The only guidance they need before the run starts is gradually to step up their level of involvement. In the first run, they can be present in the play but only take active part when they feel something is in need of prodding back on to the play's path. Once they're comfortable existing in the play's structure they can begin to take a far more active role, initiating their own interactions and possibly even discovering narrative through-lines for their character that are separate from (but enhance) the scripted play. Try to refrain from directing them during the run; a central skill of immersive work is the ability to self-correct during the performance. Notes can be given after the rehearsed section is finished, and then incorporated in the next attempt.

At this point, you're going to start to feel the lack of an audience very keenly. How you get around this depends upon your production. If some of your cast aren't utilised at certain times they can once again act as an audience, but it may be that by now you have the entire company constantly performing. If this is the case, you will need to find at least one or two adventurous souls to come and assist you, especially when you reach Phase 5.

The final part of Phase 4 are the 'What If?' Runs. These are rehearsals where the cast learn to cope with the unexpected. You, and anyone else you can draft in, should decide in advance (and in secret) how you will attempt to derail the piece. Some examples might be useful:

- In #*MSND*, what if some audience members were trying to dance with Puck when she had to apply the potion to the lovers?

- In *Caligula*, what if a sympathetic audience member tried to tell the Emperor about the senators' plotting?

- In *Loveplay*, what if an audience member steps in to try to stop the sexual assault of the Saxon woman in the forest?

Let your cast know that derailments like these will happen, but don't tell them what you'll be throwing into the mix. It's particularly important that you remain supportive; this may well be the first time an actor (even a very experienced one) has had to go through a process like this, so view this as your opportunity to help them discover tactics rather than purely a test.

Phase 5: Unifying the Strands

Your hard work has now paid off, and you have the shape of a full immersive piece of theatre. This phase is all about integrating what you have discovered into one seamless production.

The first order of business is to analyse what was discovered in the 'What If?' Runs of the previous phase, and craft your Variable Cues. We've already discussed these in-depth, so you'll have a good idea of what needs to be cued in this way within your specific piece; as a brief reminder, these are a system of multifaceted instructions that allow the cast to react to the audience without derailing the production, and you can find discussion of them in Chapter 3: Living Choices. A good rule of thumb is 'When in doubt, craft a Variable Cue.' It's far better to give your cast the safety and certainty of having planned for even the most unlikely eventualities. Ideally, this will be done individually with each cast member, because the discussion can be long and complex. While you talk privately with each of them, the rest of the cast have plenty of work to do; running scenes, speed line-runs and devising their own 'What If?' scenarios.

With the Variable Cues in place, it's time to create the Structural Outline. Gather your cast and verbally run through the structure of the piece, with everyone describing what they do in each moment. Focus entirely on the Mechanics, and don't get lost in the script at this point. Using *Anima* as an example, here's a short extract from a Structural Outline:

Case Study: Anima

DIRECTOR: Okay, the entry doors have shut and the audience have been given their briefing by Actor A.

ACTOR A: I leave the Hub through the corridor and let Actor C know that the audience will be coming in the next five minutes.

ACTOR B: I'm just outside the Hub. As soon as I see Actor A leave, I rush in and whisper to Actor D that there are terrorists in the compound.

ACTOR C: When Actor A arrives, I start the audio track in the next room, ready for the audience.

ACTOR D: When Actor B whispers to me, I cue the cast in the Hub to begin canvassing the audience to join their Faction, then leave.

ACTOR E: When Actor D gives that cue, I approach audience members who look like they could be in their fifties or older. Once I've drafted seven audience members, or fewer if it's a small audience, I ask them to join me in Actor D's room.

This is a good way of ensuring each cast member knows when they're responsible for moving the play along. It's also helpful for actors to hear in succinct terms what else is going on in the space while they're getting on with their own role.

Once everyone's comfortable, it's time for the first full run of your piece. Here's where your invited audience needs to be welcomed into the room. If you have the luxury of doing this in the performance space, run this as a proper performance but make the audience aware that this is a Mechanical run – there may be rough edges in the interactions or performances that still need finessing. Use this rehearsal efficiently, as time with an outside audience is likely to be scarce. To ensure everything is experienced, you can brief a few audience members and tell them what choices to make at certain times ('I'd like you to make sure you join up with the Osiris Corporation when you're given the chance'), but don't brief the majority. You need to see what the audience is most tempted by, so you can fix anything that proved less enticing to explore than it should be. If you have the resources, you can ask audience members to film their journeys so you can watch their experience first-hand in your own time; a smartphone camera is sufficient.

When this run is finished, prioritise your next few rehearsals according to what was discovered in this run. Rework segments that didn't happen coherently, modify or add new Variable Cues, and have a look at any Voids that cropped up. Get yourself ready for production week! If you have the time, you can Stress Test your piece; this is a combination of the audience run you've just done and a 'What If?' Run. Assign multiple audience members problematic behaviours and see how the actors cope!

Phase 6: Production Week

This phase begins when you get full access to the performance space, and replaces your traditional tech/dress/preview process – well done for getting here! There are three key rehearsals you need to set up before you're ready to open to the public. For each of these runs, you'll be glad of the Autonomous Company you've put in place; the cast and crew will have notes that you weren't able to observe by yourself.

First up, it's another Mechanical run in the space. This may have been achieved already if you've had access to the space earlier in the process, but most of you will probably need to do this now. This is a run of the piece in the space, all interaction and scenes in place, without worrying about the technical aspects. You need to ensure your cast are comfortable bringing all the work of the rehearsal room into the real space. This run should happen in real time, with each scene taking as close as possible to the actual length of time you predict.

Then it's the technical rehearsal. Your tech may be relatively similar to the Mechanical run or much more complex, depending on your production. All the usual rules apply; this is not the time to hone interactions and journeys through the space, but a time to make sure your crew are comfortable with their job. If you're combining your cast and crew, make sure your actors have their techie heads on for this run.

It might be advisable, if your piece has simultaneous scenes, to run two dress rehearsals. This lets you check on as much of the piece as you can. Other than that, a dress rehearsal is pretty much what you'd expect from any production... Except that you've got about three times as many elements to keep track of.

So far, so obvious – it's just a tech and dress with a bit of extra consideration for the immersive structure. Now, the first real test. The first night should, if you have the ability, be a preview night. Invite an audience of the vocal, the enthusiastic and the loud, along with your desired industry types (mentors and colleagues, not reviewers)! Unlike all your rehearsal runs, try not to make this one heavily based on artists you've worked with before or personal friends; you need brutal, truthful responses. Though this may sound difficult, you will reap the benefit if you can afford a whole night without a paying public. If you've done your job well, these invited guests will sell your show far more effectively than any amount of social-media marketing ever could. They will also make your show far, far better. Remember, don't invite reviewers on this occasion – that's for later.

You'll make changes to the show, if necessary, based on their experience and feedback. Opinion is divided on this, but I'd say avoid giving out those dreary feedback forms we so often see at fringe productions now. Nothing will ruin the illusion you've created quicker than a nervous-looking producer handing out clipboards and pencils after this all-consumingly visceral experience. Instead, join them on their journey. Become part of the mob, watch what they do and see what they see. You will swiftly learn how this real audience responds. You could even arrange a post-show drinks event for the audience and company to talk to each other; if you do this, an informal mingle is more enjoyable than a formal Q&A, and often leads to more fertile discussion.

Phase 7: Opening Night

And here we are... opening night! After all the work you've put in, and the rigorous testing you've gone through, this should be an incredibly exciting moment. It may well be that your immersive piece is something that's never quite been seen before; that's one of the joys of this kind of theatre.

There's nothing more to say about running this now; you've finished the hard work. Get press to your piece early, and make sure you have reviews coming thick and fast. Keep tweeting about it, and make your tweets interesting. Continue to treat your marketing the same way you treated your play; aim to turn people away from the doors by the last night.

For those of you undertaking a student production, marketing *may* not be as important a consideration, but I would encourage you to shout about what's going on from the (online) rooftops anyway. Building a visible track record of your work is always a good idea.

Good luck!

Summary of Rehearsal Phases

This is a breakdown of the seven phases of the Two-Strand Rehearsal. Obviously, there is a huge amount of work involved in the pre-production phase, so this is focused purely on working with a cast.

PHASE	CONCRETE STRAND	INTERACTIVE STRAND	GENERAL
1: Before Rehearsals			Distribute breakdowns and scripts. Establish reference points. Prepare basic immersive plans.
2: Early Exploration	Readthrough with improvised movement. Initial devising work.	Discuss the story and immersive structure. Decide on Nodes. Improvise around Nodes.	Make sure to explore the Strands in order for this phase.
3: Establishing Structure	Visit the space. Rehearse the play as with a traditional production.	Hot-seating. Entry Process. Decide on Junctions.	
4: Honing Structure	Run the play. Get feedback from an invited audience.	Bring in Floating Cast. Use 'What If?' Runs.	
5: Unifying the Strands			Variable Cues. Structural outline. Rough Mechanical run. Rework the structure. Stress Test.
6: Production Week			Mechanical run. Technical rehearsal. Dress rehearsal. Preview run. Get feedback.
7: Opening Night			Open the show!

Finding Your Niche

When you're reaching out to find an audience for your piece, remember that you're engaged in something very new. This is a lot easier to market than a faithful recreation of a Chekhov play; the easy mistake is to market it exclusively to the Chekhov crowd.

There are forms of entertainment out there that don't get a lot of media exposure but have huge numbers of devoted adherents. Look into Alternate Reality Games,[1] a community of thousands of people who spend countless hours solving interactive mysteries online and experiencing an interactive story (sound familiar?). If your piece has a historical setting, take a look at Historical Reenactment Societies and offer them a deal. If there are fantasy elements to your play, reach out to Live-Action Role-playing groups.[2] Have a look at the transmedia storytelling communities over at Inkle and Failbetter, who have been creating entire fictional versions of London and are converting classic tales like *Frankenstein* and *Around the World in Eighty Days* into interactive stories.

You're part of an emerging revolution that goes way beyond theatre; storytelling is becoming democratised. In a world inextricably entwined with social media and the interaction it brings, a reverse movement that embraces interactivity in old forms of entertainment is gaining momentum. This is where the new audiences are, and they're largely being ignored. When you're inviting theatre directors, actors and performance artists, don't forget the huge communities I mentioned above. They have just as much in common with you as the traditional theatre industry, and they're used to embracing the new and the unique.

1. A good starting point is ARGNet, a hub for this community that can be found at argn.com.
2. Groups of people who play games like Dungeons and Dragons but act it out rather than sitting round a table.

5. Living Beyond the Performance

Expanded Worlds

We live in a time where communicating with our audience outside of the theatre is easier than ever. Social media, free web hosting, cheap printing costs and open-source software that helps you achieve any creative task you can think of... All these things mean that we can open the theatrical experience up so that it begins long before the audience collect their tickets. We can also extend the experience beyond the final bow, allowing the audience to return to the world you've so skilfully crafted.

The ideas in this chapter all focus on helping you expand that experience as far as you wish. Our core concepts, Elegance and Rewards, remain crucial in this context. You don't have to engage in this kind of Expanded World-building – but if you do, it should be carried out with the same level of artistry as the performance itself. Firstly, we need to consider how these concepts apply to work done outside of the space itself.

Elegance, in this sense, means trying to keep every communication your audience receives looking like it's part of your fictional world. Rather than sending them a sheet of instructions about how *Anima* would work, we sent them propaganda and confirmation letters from the Osiris Corporation. Instead of updates on how the production was shaping up, *Caligula* allowed the audience to keep track of the machinations of the London Senate through a specially created political-news site. Keeping it all in our fictional world means that the audience has already invested in the setting by the time they reach the venue.

Rewards, here, simply mean that you better keep this interesting. Time is valuable, and the audience has already entrusted you with a couple of hours of their time for the performance itself. If you ask them to invest even more, the return on that needs to be worthwhile. You want your audience to arrive at the space salivating for more of what you've given them, not vaguely resentful at how many boring emails you've already bombarded them with.

As ever, every aspect you choose to include within your production will increase your workload exponentially. Think carefully about whether a certain kind of experience will enhance or detract from your production. In *Anima*, we engaged in a long and involved campaign before the production began, one that ran for months before the audience entered the space. In *Loveplay*, we only engaged in it to a basic level ('basic' being a relative term!). We group all of these elements under one banner: the Expanded World.

The Team

I don't know what kind of support you have access to, so while we discuss this additional work you'll need to consider *who* is going to be responsible for it. It might stay under the control of the director and producer, or you might expand the idea of the Autonomous Company to this area of the production.

It is absolutely vital to define *in advance* how you keep coherence across all the elements of the Expanded World. Someone has to have the final say, whether this is through a vote or directorial veto.

A Bonus, Not a Requirement

In the majority of cases, your audience have paid for a ticket to a single performance of your production. Anything else you add is a bonus that you offer people. As obvious as it sounds, it does carry certain pitfalls that need careful management. One fundamental mistake is making participation in the pre-show elements necessary to enjoy the show fully. Unless your audience have explicitly signed up for a multimedia event, you cannot punish them for ignoring all pre-performance communications and just engaging with the live performance.

The Expanded World should be treated as a place to explore the world and characters more fully, not as the mandatory first five chapters of the main narrative. The live production must stand alone, a complete artistic experience in its own right.

This isn't a particularly limiting rule, and there should be infinite options to explore in your Expanded World. Some starting points are listed below, but you will always have the greatest insight into what flavourful aspects of your world are fertile for further exploration.

- The backstories of characters who will be in the play.

- Events happening in the world that the main characters refer to in the live performance.

- Side stories featuring characters referred to in the play but never seen.

- Explorations that allow the audience to build a 'mental encyclopaedia' of the world.

Examples of how we've used these ideas can be found throughout this chapter.

Static and Living

In this expanded production, we think in terms of Static Tactics and Living Characters. These are measures of both how much effort the tactic demands and how much of an audience member's time it can demand.

Static Tactics are materials you generate once, probably before tickets go on sale. Once they are released, the audience has access to them and can peruse at their leisure. Examples of this include info packs sent in the post, websites and hidden treasure hunts scattered around the venue's hometown. Materials like this will be consumed at whatever pace the audience decides to approach them. This allows them to keep control over their engagement with the piece, and means that busy people aren't bombarded by your play when they don't want to be. Most importantly, however, is how it uses the traditional audience-company relationship. Material is created by the company, and consumed by the audience. Centuries of entertainment tradition means that, even when you're using something a bit more unique (like the treasure hunt), this dynamic makes it relatively easy for interested audience members to become involved.

Living Characters shake that relationship up. Just as we're experimenting with the audience-company dynamic in the space, we can experiment with it outside. By taking cues from interactive entertainment forms beyond theatre, we can create responsive worlds that live and breathe outside of one evening's performance. The basic idea of a Living Character is that the audience can interact with an entity (be it an individual or an organisation) throughout the Expanded World process. This entity will feel like a living and spontaneous personality to those interacting with it – but it will be planned and structured behind the scenes. This is, of course, the same approach that I encourage to the creation of the live performance itself. From basic tools like Twitter accounts and blogs, right the way up to multi-website fictional universes, you have the ability to invite your audience into the story before the tickets even go on sale. It's exciting and, done well, sets you apart from the crowd, but it does have the potential to alienate certain demographics. Be aware that for some people the whole concept can prove difficult to grasp, or even an unwelcome intrusion into their lives.

Static Tactics

Pre-Show Packs

One of the simplest Static Tactics is a pre-show pack, often sent out along with a purchased ticket. It's a useful way to introduce the world of the play and to create a desire to interact with the production. There's a wealth of possibilities for what you can send, but one of the most effective uses is to act as a prologue to the show.

I've used pre-show packs in three of our case-study productions, all in very different ways and on different scales. For me, it's important to ensure that any document in the pack (including, if possible, the ticket itself) feels like it came from the fictional world you're creating, and that even lists of rules and requirements are an enjoyable, artistic experience to read. You should consider each piece of paper an opportunity to market your production to your audience's friends and family. Ask yourself, with each document, whether this is something you'd want to show your friends as an audience member. If the answer is no, you can make it better. There is *nothing*, even down to the driest health and safety information, that can't be made interesting.

For two of our productions, our packs were relatively minimal. In *Loveplay*, we sent out invitations to a speed-dating event. On closer inspection, these invitations were the tickets purchased by audience members. That was enough for this play, other than a URL on the ticket that interested audience members could visit (which took them to a website for the most cheesy-looking dating agency ever conceived).

Audiences for *Caligula* received a slightly fuller info pack. An Imperial Guarantee of Free Travel, complete with wax seal, acted as their ticket. Alongside it was a certificate confirming their election as a junior senator for their local area. A quick postcode check meant that we could personalise this certificate – ensuring that they became Senators of the Grand Dioceses of Haringey, Peckham, Bethnal Green or wherever they were from. This personalisation helped the audience invest in the world and feel involved in some small way.

Where we really explored the possibilities of this tactic was *Anima*.

Case Study: Anima

I mentioned how you can make the driest information interesting in its own right. We explored that in depth with *Anima*, our most complex play in terms of structure. Upon buying their tickets, audience members received a thick tan envelope. Inside it were various documents. Some of them were necessary for the show to function: tickets, rules for the performance, health and safety information, time and location of the performance… Others were purely for artistic, flavourful reasons.

In that pack, the audience received the following:

Welcome Letter

This thanked the audience member for signing up to the Osiris Corporation's 'Disaster Insurance Policy'. There followed a precis of the other materials in the pack, and some corporate buzzspeak about the work of the corporation.

ID Badge

The tickets were turned into small paper ID badges. On the badge was the audience member's name, a code representing their 'membership package' (more on which later), the logo of the Osiris Corporation and a meaningless string of letters and numbers. They were paperclipped to the welcome letter, with an instruction to display them prominently when they arrived for orientation.

Orientation Session Invitation

Audience members were told that their 'training drill' would occur at the date and location of the live show. They were told attendance was mandatory, with loss of their insurance policy at stake. The tone was cold and instructional, building the dictatorial image of Osiris. Health and safety rules were given, along with spurious in-world reasons for them.

Membership Level

A list of six levels of insurance, with one highlighted at random. Audience members could be anything from Alpha Plus to Omega (Economy Lite), and read what they were entitled to in the event of an apocalyptic disaster. Alpha Plus offered immediate relocation to a luxury apartment in an S3 (see below), a choice of jobs and financial and material support for five years after the disaster. Omega (Economy Lite), on the other hand, offered assignment to an Osiris Industrial Complex with a preselected manual job, one basic food package a day and the opportunity to earn credits to eventually move to an S3. Reading the small print would make clear that the lowest-budget accommodation in an S3 would require seventeen years' worth of credits.

These membership levels, displayed on their badges, would dictate how audience members were treated on arriving at the performance. Being ushered through to the waiting area and given a drink awaited the highest members, whilst Omegas found themselves subjected to a gruelling medical and psychological evaluation. These differences continued throughout the play. We had a lot of fun deciding whether a group booking would receive equal membership levels or be treated differently.

S3 Brochure

A stapled booklet of four futuristic-looking cities, with estate-agent-style language explaining the comfort and style that post-apocalyptic living could bring. This had no function in the play, and was merely there to provide Flavour.

Other than providing the required information in an interesting way, the info pack served some hidden functions for us. By assigning different membership levels, we promoted discussion between audience members who wished to understand why they'd been allocated these levels – and what it might mean for the performance. Our Twitter feed began buzzing with conversations about it, marketing the show to people we wouldn't otherwise reach. This meant that, with an advertising budget of zero and no real track record, we sold out five weeks before opening. Looking at the numbers made it clear that surges in sales accompanied tweets and Facebook posts from those who'd received their info packs.

Not only that, but the audience arrived in the space already having questions and interest in the world. We were able to remove huge amounts of expository world-building from the performance itself and dive straight into the story. Given that we were building a very complex scenario, this was vital for the energy of the piece.

Websites

If you're a professional company, it goes without saying that you have a web presence for your company. If you don't, then go and sort that out *immediately*. I'll wait here and pretend I didn't notice. At a minimum, get yourself a website (WordPress is a great option for quickly building affordable yet professional sites), a Facebook page and a Twitter account. You may also have a web presence for the production itself. Events on Facebook, links to ticketing sites, press links...

These are all useful things to have, but they're not what we're talking about here. We're going to deal with the web presence of your fictional world, which is a separate entity to your traditional online marketing strategies. We'll leave social media aside for now, as these fall squarely into the Living Characters category.

Those of you still studying or in training can use the web tactics we're about to discuss even if you're not marketing the show in the usual sense. You may not be allowed to sell tickets to the world outside your school or university, but that doesn't necessarily affect the Expanded World you can create.

Any aspect of your show can have a web presence and, as with our pre-show packs, they can be used to add depth and Flavour to your performance before the evening begins. There are, however, a number of aspects to consider before you start. The first of these is your audience reach.

The harder your audience has to work to access something, the fewer of them will explore it. It may sound like obvious advice, but it goes hand in hand with a more nebulous concept: not all things are equally difficult to all people. When we talk about online material, we're automatically skewing the target age range downwards. This isn't a hard-and-fast rule, and older generations are becoming increasingly tech-savvy as time goes on. Competent, however, doesn't necessarily translate into enthusiastic. Bear your audience in mind, then, when you design the web presence for your world.

When we call this tactic 'Static', that doesn't refer to how the experience *feels* to the audience member – it's in reference to our level of effort. We build it, and then it maintains itself without needing manual updating by us. When we build Static web tactics, we want the audience to feel like they're getting the level of interactivity they'll receive in our productions. To make this happen, we make sure they stick to at least one of two concepts: Responsive and Progressive.

Responsive means that the audience feels like they can interact with the site and receive some kind of personalised experience. This usually comes from setting up a site to request certain information from a user then responding using that data to modify the output. There are many time-worn and boring ways to do this. Having an email list that sends out the same mail to everyone but uses the audience member's name... well, that's what email spammers have been doing for years. We can be far more creative than that.

Case Study: Loveplay

In *Loveplay*, we wanted to build something that evoked the feeling of signing up to a dating website. We trawled various sites like OKCupid and Match.com to get a feel for the kind of questions asked of new visitors, and set to work building our own. By using a great free tool called Typeform (easily searchable on Google) we were able to build a professional-looking questionnaire. It also automatically compiles your results, allowing the participant to view them in a pretty visual format.

The questions we asked started out standard... Name, age, job, all of that usual data. Then we started, gradually, injecting what made our world unique. When asking about the ideal partner, the choices offered varied from 'rugged and muscular with a horned helmet' to 'quiet and sensitive, ideally with a top hat and pocket watch'. When asked where they'd most like to go on holiday, they could pick from a list that included 'a longboat sailing past the Norwegian fjords' and 'the Imperial City herself'. On completing the questionnaire, they were matched with their ideal partner of the preferred gender. A surprising number ended up with Oláf Sigürdson, but Dame Charlotte Pendleton-Smythe also proved popular.

This done, an email was automatically sent to the audience member with more details on their match, and the location and date of their meeting (conveniently, the exact same details as the performance they were booked for...). The audience arrived with a prior understanding of the world we'd built and a personal investment – some even hunted out their matches from our Floating Cast, in effect creating new scenes for our production!

Now you may be thinking that as a Responsive website requires input from the audience, it falls under the category of a Living Character rather than a Static Tactic. The difference is in the level of upkeep required on our part. We were able to set up the questionnaire and the automatic emails before the site went live. Audience members could interact with it and receive communication in response without us having to take an active part after that initial set-up. The best Static Tactics are ones that feel Responsive and interactive despite being totally predefined.

Progressive web tactics are ones that provide more and more content as time goes on. The most basic format of this is a blog; a site that can be revisited again and again to see the next instalment in the story. What keeps this a Static Tactic is that all content can be written and queued up before the first audience member ever clicks your link.

We explored this tactic in both *Caligula* and *Anima*. The first ideas that sprang to mind when considering updatable content are generally mailing lists and blogs, but in both cases we wanted to think a little further outside of the box. We started by discussing our fictional worlds and identifying all the people and organisations within them who might have a web presence of any kind. In *Anima*, we had two clear contenders: the Osiris Corporation, and the Network. Looking further afield, we could conceive of a news site following the developments in their quarrel. We could also come up with more and more obscure ideas, such as a group of religious extremists predicting the end of the world or a community of (what seemed to be) conspiracy theorists investigating Osiris. *Caligula* inspired suggestions such as a website for the Imperial Senate, the office of the Emperor, a political-news site and a network of dissidents agitating for a return to Republican rule (as our setting had been updated to a dystopian London, there was no problem with the Empire having a web presence!). With each of these ideas, we planned in advance how content would roll out over a period of time before the production (thus making them Progressive).

Have a think, and see what groups suggest themselves from your production. Work outwards, starting from those that are directly represented in your performance – possibly with half an eye on the Factions you might end up creating. When you've explored those to their fullest extent, have fun building an Expanded World that supports your performance. What groups could conceivably exist and add Flavour to your piece, even if they are never referenced in the event itself?

Having done this, divide these groups into three categories. Firstly, groups that you want to be a focal point for your Expanded World. These websites could publish several new batches of content as time rolls on to the opening night. The second category is for groups that are potentially interesting, but don't need a huge amount of time poured into them. They would receive no more than a couple of updates, possibly none at all beyond their initial content. Lastly, those that just don't seem worth the work in the first place. Note that, at this point, you've not decided what shape their web presence will take, merely that they're fertile ground for exploration.

With this done, start exploring how these groups will display themselves to the audience. Try to keep a good variety going rather than just giving each group a blog or mailing list. There's a wealth of options here, and the list only grows every year as the internet matures. YouTube channels, WordPress sites, Tumblr blogs, Mailchimp lists, SoundCloud accounts and more can all be explored. Choosing the right format for each group comes from considering how this group would want to communicate. A faceless corporation is more likely to have a website or mailing list than a blog. An individual may have a YouTube channel, but probably not a mailing list. We end up with a list of Outlets (an Outlet being a self-contained corner of the internet) along with how much input each will have.

Case Study: Caligula

In *Caligula*, we ended up with the following Outlets:

- The Imperial Senate's WordPress site, with sanitised political news and propaganda (minimal updates), used purely to create the illusion of the Senate existing before the performance and to mention the names of characters from the play. It was designed to help the audience connect with the setting immediately upon entering the production venue.

- The WordPress site of the Offices of the Emperor. This deliberately received no updates at all, the intention being to promote the idea that the Emperor was distant and out-of-touch with the public.

- The mailing list used by the Republican dissidents (minimal updates). This fired out emails on roughly the same schedule as the Senate's site updates. The mails provided an alternative perspective on the Senate's business, leading our audience to become aware of the rifts in the Empire. We wanted them to arrive expecting intrigue and political scheming.

- An amateur Imperial historian's Tumblr blog (regular updates). This was a purely Flavour site that rewrote the early Roman Empire's history to fit our dystopian London setting. This had two purposes – first, to help the audience understand the context within which *Caligula* existed. Knowing the preceding history of Rome (from Julius Caesar to Nero) would enhance enjoyment of the play, so we hoped to do this in a vibrant and enjoyable way. Secondly, by replacing references to Imperial Rome with contemporary London personalities and locations, we wanted to encourage the audience to invest more of themselves and their opinions into the play. We reasoned that they would be more likely to reveal their true thoughts about matters such as religion, immigration, privacy and the economy if the setting was one they recognised as home. It seemed to work; the audience were much more invested than I anticipated, and I have to assume that touches like this made a difference.

Case Study: Anima

Anima ended up spawning just two regularly updated Outlets:

- The WordPress site for the Osiris Corporation (regular updates). This gradually introduced characters from the play along with building the narrative. Eagle-eyed audience members worked out that the 'wonder drug' being developed eventually caused the plague that underpinned the whole play.

- The Network's blog (regular updates). This gave hints as to the sinister nature of Osiris, but also made clear that the Network were themselves incredibly ruthless and manipulative. These two sites together were designed to create uncertainty and paranoia when the audience found themselves caught between both groups in the performance.

Different Objectives for Outlets

You may have noticed that the functions of our Expanded Worlds in those two plays differed slightly. In *Caligula*, we engaged in world-building and background stories, but none of this fed directly into the narrative of the performance itself. In *Anima*, on the other hand, we were telling an extended story, and audience members following the online elements experienced the live performance as the climactic chapter in a three-month-long story. You can assign whatever purpose you like to your Expanded World, but remember to make it optional. This is an addition to your play, and the audience must be able to enjoy the live performance in isolation if they so choose.

It's worth remembering that some audience members may book only a short time before the production, or even buy tickets on the door. Give some thought to what experience these people can have with your Expanded World. For *Anima*, we decided to leave the web presence live for a long time after the production had ended so that latecomers could delve deeper into the background (with the exception of certain Responsive elements that would have been either completed or rendered redundant by the events of the production). Viewing these sites after the performance didn't have the drip-feed of new content that the Progressive updates and Responsive elements normally provided, but it did allow a window into this larger experience. It also provides an incentive to book earlier next time. 'Enjoyed the experience? Next time, you could enjoy it for two months!'

We kept the pre-show packs exclusive to those who booked in enough time to have them sent. There's nothing wrong with creating a bit of exclusivity and excitement around your production...

Planning Your Presence

If you're going to use Static tactics with periodic updates, it's a very good idea to write *all* of the content in advance – ideally, before the first piece of it goes live. The vast majority of Outlets allow you to schedule posts, and free tools like Google Calendar allow you to share a visual timetable of those posts with all the relevant team members. This is very simple to set up. We tended to assign each Outlet a colour in Google Calendar, and make an event in that colour whenever a post is scheduled. It is *crucial* that everything is hosted in the cloud somewhere (Dropbox, for example), rather than on a team member's computer. If someone's laptop dies, you don't want it taking half the Expanded World with it.

Later in this chapter, we talk through some free tools that can streamline the maintenance of your Expanded World even further.

Item Drops

Item Drops can be an exciting addition to an Expanded World, especially if your audience is largely centred in a big urban area. This takes its cues from geocaching, a worldwide collaborative treasure hunt, and it's deceptively simple to carry out and understand. Essentially, you secrete an object related to your play in a hidden location, and release clues to the audience that help them find it. The task falls into two parts: deciding how to give out the clues and placing the chosen object. We'll start with the hiding place itself.

The first consideration is that it needs to be legal. You need to obtain the permission of the landowner (technically, this is true even of tiny, unobtrusive objects); whether it's in a shop window or buried underground, it's almost certain that you're encroaching on someone's property. If that's an individual or small business, it may be a case of just talking to them in person and seeing if they're up for it. On public land, such as pavements or town squares, the local council is probably your first port of call. Once permission is given, you need to ensure the treasure hunt is safe. Put yourself in the audience's place – would they be at risk during their search? Having them ferreting around on a narrow pavement by a busy road is a recipe for disaster, and presents severe legal problems if something unpleasant happens. Your ideal location is going to be somewhere that straddles the fine line between too obvious and too obscure. If you want some examples, heading to the geocaching website (conveniently located at geocaching.com) will show you where your nearest treasure hunts are. Try a few of them out and get a feel for how they work.

The object itself will be dictated by both the location and the live production. One common object in urban geocaching are small magnetic cylinders with scrolls of paper inside. These are very affordable, and easy to place discreetly. Inside can be hidden messages from characters, documents about the organisations in your world or anything else you can conceive of. One tactic we played with for *Anima* was placing a URL on there that couldn't be found anywhere else within our Expanded World. Our fictional justification was that these hidden cylinders were dead drops for Network agents to communicate with each other, and the links took audience members to unlisted YouTube videos with leaked footage from Osiris meetings. For larger objects, you'll need somewhere that won't be cleaned up by a dutiful citizen! We've tended to shy away from larger drops, but we're primarily based in London where space is at a premium! If you're somewhere more conducive to large troves, the field is wide open for you to experiment with different objects.

It's very important to remember that this level of effort will only be undertaken by a small section of your audience. This brings you two responsibilities in choosing the object. Firstly, these item drops cannot be, *in any way*, vital to enjoying the play. However, those valiant few who *do* undertake the search had better receive a very satisfying Reward for their efforts. Make sure that whatever they find is well worth the time they've given. Reward them with insights and connections that open up the Expanded World in unexpected ways.

As for the clues themselves, these can be given out in any number of ways. We've already discussed some possible vehicles for disseminating the directions, so you can use pre-show packs and your web presence to do this. You can also use the Living Characters we'll discuss next as your method. As always, make this Elegant. The clues should come through the story, not from your theatre company announcing that there is a treasure hunt for audience members.

Living Characters

Permissions

Before we explore Living Characters, a blanket piece of advice. Many of these methods involve using contact details given to you by audience members to communicate with them. These could include email addresses, phone numbers or home addresses. If any of these are being used for your Expanded World, you must get *explicit* permission to contact them via these methods for that purpose. Just because an audience member gave you their email address to send their ticket receipt, don't assume this means you can start sending them Expanded World material. You are legally obliged to gain permission for this, but even if you weren't, it would still make sense. You don't want people complaining about being harassed when all you're trying to do is give them more value for their ticket's money.

There's a difference between 'opting in' and 'opting out' of the Expanded World. Imagine that, on your online box office, you've put a checkbox underneath where your audience member puts their email address. If this says 'Please tick this box if you *do not* wish to receive additional story materials from the production', you are giving them the ability to opt out of the Expanded World. For legal purposes, this would suffice. As long as that option was presented on the same page that asks for their email address, you have obeyed the law (though you're also supposed to include an unsubscribe link on all subsequent emails to be fully compliant). I personally don't think this is enough, and I recommend you get people to *opt in* to the story – if the box stays unticked, they don't take part. For bonus ethical Brownie points, you can give them the option to opt in to each different means of communications: yes to emails, yes to texts, etc. There is a limit, though... Put too many tick boxes on the form, and some audience members will find you just as irritating as if you'd never sought permission at all.

You want the audience's goodwill. Making your experience opt-in will ensure that only people who really want the Expanded World will receive it. If you're worried about people missing that checkbox and feeling left out, make sure there's a prominent link on your company's website and Facebook page allowing them to opt in at a later date. This is far, far better than receiving angry emails from a technologically illiterate and very angry audience member who insists they never wanted emails from you and would now like a refund on their ticket. Luckily, this hasn't happened to me – but I know a few people who've experienced it.

What are Living Characters?

Living Characters are fantastic. If you have the time (they take a lot of time), the energy (they require quite a bit of energy...) and the discipline (oh so much discipline) then... then...

Let me start again. Living Characters are an incredible burden. They require constant upkeep, a disciplined approach, huge amounts of planning, the ability to manage problems on the fly, and a compelling storyline. They are not to be undertaken lightly. They present big challenges, but they can reap big rewards. They are not necessary for the health of your play, and they can't make a mediocre production better. But if you have the stomach for all that, and if your core performance is going to be watertight... then let's play.

Living Characters give the audience a true two-way communication with the Expanded World. They may enter conversation with characters who respond to their questions. Living Characters are the embodiment of our immersive ideas liberated from the performance space. We approach them, therefore, in a very different way to our Static Tactics.

With Static methods, we talked in terms of methods and Outlets. Every tactic was a discrete, self-contained channel: a treasure hunt, an info pack, a website. These things may interlink, but they exist in isolation. Even if two Outlets are run by the same fictional group (say, a website and a mailing list both owned by the same fictional company), they operate independently of each other according to a predefined timetable. The Living Character has to be much more holistic than this.

We begin from a similar starting point: highlighting individuals from the world of the production who would provide interesting interactions for the audience. Unlike Static Tactics, Living Characters should be represented as individuals rather than groups. If you wish to use a company or organisation for a Living Character, create a position within that group. A minister, executive marketing manager or baron has an individual voice – a company or government just has buzzwords and propaganda. I would advise you not to use more than two or three unique voices. Each one requires a huge amount of work, and one effectively used Living Character is worth far more than seven poorly executed ones. Try to avoid using characters from the performance itself, as studying all previous communication with audience members and memorising it would be a hefty task for the actor, who already has quite enough to deal with as part of the live interactive production.

So: identify your voices.

Narrative Thrust

To be effective, a Living Character should be given a well-written Narrative Thrust. This is made up of two elements. First, their Arc; a compelling story that the audience can uncover by communicating with them. By the end of their time with the character, audience members should feel like they've discovered a truly fascinating plotline that would otherwise have stayed hidden. Secondly, their Function. This is the purpose they serve you as a theatre-maker, what they bring to the Expanded World that can't be achieved through Static means.

Quite often, the Arc will come naturally once you've decided their Function. For example, we decided that one Living Character's Function was 'To unbalance the audience and cause them to distrust the main characters.' Another's was 'To help the audience invest in their assigned Faction by giving them a reason to care about it.' That first example was drawn from *Anima*. We ended up deciding the Living Character was a disgruntled ex-Network terrorist. She had valid reason to hate both power groups in the performance, and audience members who engaged with her would discover her history, as well as being given access to hidden weblinks of Network correspondence and secret Osiris projects. These links, a substantial Reward for adventurous audience members, helped further her Function whilst also giving her a distinct story and narrative. Our second example appeared in the Expanded World for *Caligula*. We designed them as a gossipy seneschal, on hand to help new junior senators navigate the murky intrigues of the Senate. He solicited their opinions on important matters and discussed the political landscape of the court with them, a useful way of introducing main characters from the play without having to use them directly as Living Characters.

We found that, with these and our other Living Characters, a surprising number of the audience enjoyed interacting with them. On average, about sixty per cent would engage and interact with them to some level. Just over a quarter of the audience explored their storylines to their conclusion. Whilst this isn't a huge number, it transpired that if an audience member got that far, they became one of our greatest marketing tools. In two of our case-study productions, we discovered Facebook groups and Twitter hashtags had spontaneously sprung up for audience members to talk to each other about their interactions. As we had made sure to personalise the contact between the Living Character and each participant, they were able to share their unique experiences. The greatest payoff for us was that audience members would sometimes initiate contact with Living Characters *after* the live performance – the story meant enough to them that they wanted to find closure with the character they'd spent weeks (in some cases) talking to.

You might find it useful – once the Narrative Thrust is decided – to give each Living Character a snappy moniker that serves as a shorthand for understanding their through-line: Gossipy Seneschal, Disgruntled Activist, Paranoid Scientist, etc., etc....

Living Communication

It goes without saying that most of the methods used in Static Tactics can work for your Living Characters too. There are also a lot of other avenues open to you, some of which can really elevate your Living Characters into incredible audience experiences.

As long as you gained the relevant permissions from your audience, tools exist online that allow you to send text messages via the internet. This kind of communication automatically takes audiences into new territory. We are very used to being marketed to by emails and websites – a personally worded text will bring the Living Character into a more real life. Make sure any emails actively solicit the audience member's personal response, so that the reader realises this is a real two-way communication. Services also exist that allow you to record voice messages – and the website then phones the audience member with this message. It's a good idea to reserve these more interesting (but also more intrusive) methods for later on in the Living Character's Arc. Any audience member who reaches that stage of the story has proven themselves invested enough to welcome these new variations.

You can draw out a flowchart of the Living Character's timeline; we find this helps us visualise the audience's 'journey'. Each step in the chart is a 'chapter' of the story – a piece of information the Living Character will reveal, or a question they might ask the audience, which is also assigned a method of communication. Our Gossipy Seneschal explored his first few chapters via email before discussing more sensitive matters by text. Laying it out like this also allows you to branch out their Arc – there may be audience members who don't want phone communication, so you plot out a parallel branch of the Living Character experience using different methods only.

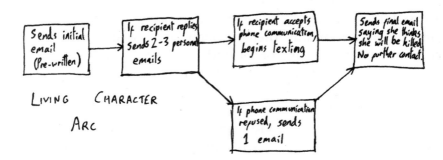

Given that this is a more complex area than simple websites and mailing lists, it may seem strange that we leave this section here – but frankly there's no way to cover infinite possibilities. Imagine how your Living Character would operate in real life, and scour the internet for free tools that allow you to replicate this.

Linking Your Tactics

While each method we've discussed can be incredibly effective in isolation, their 'wow' factor explodes when you interlink them. When a Static Tactic feeds into a Living Character, who in turn feeds back to another website, you create a living network of stories that the audience can get lost in. The great news for you is that interweaving them in this way actually *decreases* the amount of time you spend maintaining Living Characters. If interacting with your Living Character sends the audience off to explore a chain of Static Tactics that you've made in advance, the story manages itself for a while. An example of this sort of chain could be useful...

Imagine one of the first Static Tactics your audience encounters is a website. This website belongs to a research group (or a university, or an army, or a government, or a dating agency, or a knitting circle...) and, whilst trawling the site, the viewer encounters a page that asks if they want to join the group. They do, indeed, want to join. They click the link, and get taken to a Typeform which asks them questions about themselves and their reasons for joining. Their answers generate a personalised result, with the promise that they'll be contacted soon. A day or so later, they receive an email from a Living Character. During this conversation, the Living Character sends them an invite to a private Facebook group. The audience member then spends a happy couple of days exploring this and interacting with their fellow audience members, punctuated by occasional email contact with the Living Character. But at some point, a new Living Character contacts them. They've 'noticed them' on the new site, and are looking for allies in exposing some dark secret at the heart of the group. If interested, they're given clues to an item drop somewhere, within which is a link to a further Static website... and so on.

Describing it verbally like that can be overwhelming, but when we represent it visually...

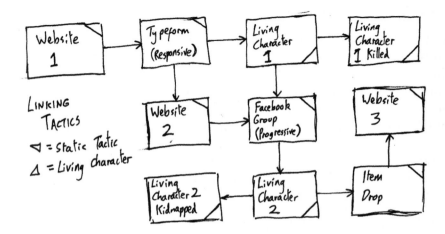

You'll notice that only small elements of that chain require active maintenance by the company... But due to its variety, it feels far more living and 'real' than a two-week long conversation with a Living Character. The example above is simple, with one through-line. You'll swiftly grow confident enough to add subplots and branches. Eventually, you may end up offering as much freedom of choice within this Expanded World as you will within the live performance.

As your content expands, you need tools to keep track of everything and make sure the Living Characters are responding to the right audience members at the right time. There are two sites that will make this incredibly simple, both free. The first is Buffer (bufferapp.com), a site that allows you to link various social-media accounts on one dashboard, and schedule posts months in advance. This makes running Twitter accounts and Facebook pages incredibly simple, and also allows multiple people to share those accounts easily.

The other is IFTTT (ifttt.com). This tool didn't exist when we first started playing with Living Characters, and since discovering it we have cut down our maintenance time by an incredible amount. IFTTT stands for 'If This Then That', and it allows you to create 'recipes' to make things happen on various sites you own. Every recipe takes the format 'IF something happens THEN something else will happen.' For example, 'IF someone follows this Twitter account THEN send them an email.'

This can automate chains (like the one in the flowchart). Imagine if merely the act of completing the Typeform could automatically cue an introductory email from the Gossipy Seneschal to initiate contact with the audience member. Rather than manually trawling through the Typeform each day to see new responses, you could sit back and wait for people to reply to the email they've been sent. IFTTT can operate on your phone too, even to the extent of changing your phone's background picture if a certain thing happens (as well as sending more standard alerts and notifications). And if someone's getting close to the end of a chain of Static sites, a notification can appear on your phone. This gives you time to prepare for interacting with the individual audience member again without constantly monitoring everyone's progress.

Non-Theatre Audiences

If you're building a quite extensive Expanded World, there's a further opportunity to market your show. Alternate Reality Games (ARGs) have been existing online for the better part of twenty-five years, and they use exactly the kind of methods we're talking about here. Exposing ARG communities to your Expanded World provides a great opportunity to market your production to a group who would never normally hear of your work. As well as your production leading audiences to the Expanded World, the reverse can be true. The Expanded World can lead previously inaccessible audiences to your work – and maybe they'll even buy a ticket!

Now, bear in mind that these communities have been engaging in activities like this for years. They are used to sophisticated and fully planned worlds that operate without a hitch. Whilst they don't use this word, they are used to fully Elegant games to play in. So if you're going to go there, make sure your world is of the quality they would enjoy.

Entry to ARGs is normally achieved through 'trailheads' – obscure clues that lead players down the rabbit hole of your world. They're used to working hard for the clues, and it's not uncommon to have URLs in code, or scrambled in mixed-up audio files, so you can have fun creating this for them if you want. Remember, though, that ARG players will not automatically care about your production. They're used to discovering, somewhere along the line, that the ARG is marketing a product – but the more fun they've had before discovering this, the more likely they are to purchase a ticket.

Checklist

Here's a checklist of the concepts we've covered in this book as a useful reference tool that will help you plan and rehearse your immersive production, and the pages where they first appear:

1. Starting Out

2. Living Spaces

3. Living Choices

Everything is at your disposal. Having read this book, you now know how to:

- Use the space to send the audience on breakneck journeys punctuated by unexpected moments of stillness and claustrophobia.

- Set scenes in appropriate locations, and know why those locations are appropriate.

- Assign the audience a role in which they'll enjoy investing.

- Manage the production and ensure that freedom of action never derails the artistic experience at its heart.

- Make the most of your rehearsal time, and the company who shares it with you.

- Expand the play beyond the space, bursting into the homes and lives of the audience.

All that's missing from the puzzle is your own personal vision. This book provides some techniques and starting points – now you need to provide the spark to bring it all to life by creating your own world.

I wish you the greatest luck in the challenging and exciting journey you're beginning. I'll see you there.

Glossary

Arc The individual subplot of a Living Character. Combines with the Function to create Narrative Thrust.

Autonomous Company A cast and crew that can take joint responsibility for building the world with the director.

Background Pull The inherent Pull possessed by the Zones in a space before you interfere with them.

Boundary A physical or subconscious barrier that defines distinct Zones.

Boundary (*Action*) Creating boundaries through interaction.

Boundary (*Light*) Using light and shadow to create boundaries.

Boundary (*Physical*) Using physical objects as boundaries.

Dispersing the Audience Creating a stimulus for the audience to leave the area via multiple exits. A form of Dividing the Audience. See also Shaving and Splitting.

Dividing the Audience Using Flow or the play's action to discourage your audience from congregating in one group. See Splitting, Shaving, Dispersing and Extracting.

Elegance The idea that an immersive piece should keep its Mechanics hidden, and that everything (even health and safety briefings) should feel like part of the fictional world.

Entry Process The 'scene' that audience members encounter when they first arrive at your production. Vital for setting your Rules of Engagement.

Expanded World Interactive storytelling that occurs before the live performance as part of your production. Primarily created with Static Tactics and Living Characters.

Extracting the Audience Sending audience members down a new Path without their active choice. See also Dividing the Audience, Forced Choice and Implied Choice.

Factions The character/story roles assigned to the audience in immersive productions.

Features The unique attributes of a space that can be used to your advantage. See also Space (Denying the) and Space (Incorporating the).

Flavour Describing the elements of the play that are purely there to provide your fictional world with a feeling of scope and depth.

Floating Cast The cast members who join the process later in the rehearsal period. Their primary function is to help the interactive elements run smoothly rather than play main characters.

Flow The inherent qualities of a multi-Zoned space and how they facilitate or hinder journeys through it. See also Pull.

Forced Choice Overtly giving the audience a multiple choice of Paths to take. See also Extracting the Audience and Implied Choice.

Freedoms The abilities we give our audience during the production. These can include freedom of movement and freedom to Influence the story.

Function The purpose a Living Character serves in the Expanded Play. Combines with the Arc to create Narrative Thrust.

Funnel   A Zone that encourages the audience to move through it. See also Void.

Gravity   The idea that the audience will be attracted to Boundaries and objects rather than empty spaces.

Hub   A Zone where the audience is likely to congregate and feel a sense of safety; by default, the Zone with the highest Pull.

Immersive Additions   The elements added to a pre-existing scripted play that allow audience Freedoms.

Impact   How hard your company has to work to deal with a specific interaction. See also Influence.

Implied Choice   Giving the audience a free choice of Path without explicitly explaining their options. See also Extracting the Audience and Forced Choice.

Influence   How much Impact a particular interaction can have on the narrative of the play. See also Impact.

Junctions   The points in the play where audience choice can shift the narrative. See also Paths and Threads.

Living Characters   Part of the Expanded World. Fictional characters with whom the audience can interact virtually prior to the live performance. See also Static Tactics.

Mechanical Runs   Rehearsals that focus purely on the Mechanics of the interactions.

Mechanics   The underlying systems you put in place to manage interactions, such as Variable Cues and Factions.

Mission Statement   Your guiding objective when creating immersive theatre.

Narrative Thrust   The guidelines for using a Living Character, comprising their Arc and their Function.

Nodes   The key events that must occur in the production for the narrative to progress. A concept integral to the Two-Strand Rehearsal.

Outlets Small 'areas' of the internet (such as websites) used as Static Tactics.

Paths The individual story routes that audience members take in between Junctions. Though they may have freedom of action during a Path, they will be unable to change the fundamental course of the play. See also Junctions and Threads.

Progressive An online Static Tactic that provides periodic updates to keep audiences interested (such as a blog).

Pull The factors a particular Zone possesses that dictate how strongly the audience will gravitate towards it. Also used to denote how objects *within* a Zone exert Gravity. See also Flow.

Push An action or quality that encourages the audience to leave the space. See also Dispersing the Audience and Funnel.

Region A linked group of Zones that encourage exploring between them. They often share sightlines or a central connecting corridor.

Responsive An online Static Tactic that appears to adapt itself to the audience's actions (e.g. an automatic welcome email that uses data from a questionnaire completed by the audience member).

Rewards Anything that makes an audience member feel like exploring or interacting was worth their time. It can be an overheard conversation, an object, a new scene or anything else you can conceive.

Rules Bloat Burdening players with excess rules in Game Theatre.

Rules of Engagement The unspoken code of conduct that your production operates under. They dictate how audiences can interact and what is expected of them.

Shaving the Audience Encouraging a small group of more adventurous audience members to explore further afield. A form of Dividing the Audience. See also Dispersing and Splitting the Audience.

Social Pull A factor that grows throughout the production, representing the audience's tendency to stay with other people they've identified as safe or pleasant company. See also Pull.

Space (*Denying the*) Attempting to mould an unsuitable space into the setting you've imagined.

Space (*Incorporating the*) Combining the pre-existing space with the emotional tone you wish to achieve. The result may be a different setting to the one you imagined.

Splitting the Audience Breaking the audience into groups of roughly equal size. A form of Dividing the Audience. See also Dispersing and Shaving the Audience.

Static Tactics Part of the Expanded World. Refers to ready-made elements that the audience can explore at leisure without active maintenance from the company. See also Living Characters.

Stress Test A rehearsal where the company test the Mechanics of the production to their limits so that they can identify flaws in the Mechanical design.

Structural Outline An exercise where the company talk through the Mechanics of the play chronologically.

Sync Points Scenes specifically designed to bring Paths together and synchronise different parts of the production.

Threads Routes that the production can take as it gets influenced by the audience's Freedoms. See also Paths and Junctions.

Two-Strand Rehearsal A rehearsal process that keeps the scripted (Concrete Strand) and immersive (Interactive Strand) elements of the play separate until later in the process.

Variable Cues A process of creating multiple trigger events to begin the next section of the production. This allows actors to adapt to changing circumstances whilst keeping the play on track.

Void A Zone that discourages the audience from exploring and which dampens the atmosphere. See also Funnel.

Void (*Forcing the*) Planning your space to ensure a Void emerges.

Void (*Smashing the*) Planning your space to ensure Voids don't emerge.

'What If?' Runs   Rehearsals where the actors are presented with unexpected interactions in order to hone their ability to respond to all possibilities. This is an element of the Two-Strand Rehearsal.

Zone   An area within the space that shares a Boundary.

Acknowledgements

Writing this book was only possible thanks to the support of my friends, family and collaborators, along with the work of artists who pioneered immersive theatre long before I set my sights on it.

The companies I reference in the text have pushed the form forwards through the years. Many thanks, therefore, to Punchdrunk, You Me Bum Bum Train and OneOhOne. Particular gratitude goes to Jamie Harper at Hobo Theatre, and Stephen and Suzi Israel at The Company for allowing me insight and access to their processes.

This book would be infinitely less honed and readable without the incredible efforts and support of Matt Applewhite, my editor at Nick Hern Books.

For my work with AXIS Arts, particular thanks to those who laboured alongside me and dealt with my maniacal ambitions. There are too many names to mention here, but some in particular stand out: Emma Pritchard and Rosie Frecker uncomplainingly acted as Executive Producers on many projects, including #MSND which was directed by the visionary Will Davis. Nick Bradford was along for every step of that journey, and now leads AXIS Arts in New York. Jessica-Lee Hopkins starred in #MSND and continues to suffer long after the curtain dropped on that show by agreeing to be my housemate and listen/playtest my many ridiculous ideas.

Dylan Mason helped me create *Anima* and was an instrumental force in the genesis of many of the concepts in this book. Anna Micheli, meanwhile, became my sounding board and quality filter when I started exploring ideas for *Caligula* while we studied in Moscow. Alexandra Shaw was my designer and co-conspirator on *Loveplay*, and her work was pivotal in creating the piece. Andrea Brooks, Tony Clark and Steve Hallam all helped usher me over the threshold from student to professional, and I am indebted to their patience and belief.

Big thanks to the delightful cities of Dubrovnik, Istanbul and Annecy, where parts of this book were written. Thanks as well to the Layhe family, who took me there!

Finally, the most constant and long-suffering support structure that is my family (both by blood and choice). To my four parents (Michelle, Kevin, Nick and Claire), four brothers (Max, Joe, Ollie and Harry), one girlfriend (Harriet, who is simply the best human being in existence in any universe), eleven rats ('the girls'), two cats ('the boys') and one dog ('the Snoot')... Thank you. You have no idea how much I love you all.

Finally, to those of you who've read this book... I hope you've enjoyed it and found it useful. I would love to hear from you, about the results of your work or new concepts you've hit upon. You can find me on Twitter as @AxisCarthage.

www.nickhernbooks.co.uk

facebook.com/nickhernbooks

twitter.com/nickhernbooks